HOW TO GET THE FINANCING FOR YOUR NEW SMALL BUSINESS:

Innovative Solutions from the Experts Who Do It Every Day

By Sharon Fullen

How to Get the Financing for Your New Small Business:
Innovative Solutions from the Experts Who Do It Every Day

Copyright © 2006 by Atlantic Publishing Group, Inc.

1210 SW 23rd Place • Ocala, Florida 34474 • 800-814-1132 • 352-622-5836–Fax

Web site: www.atlantic-pub.com • E-mail sales@atlantic-pub.com

SAN Number :268-1250

ISBN-13: 978-0-910627-55-9

ISBN-10: 0-910627-55-X

Library of Congress Cataloging-in-Publication Data

Fullen, Sharon L.
  How to get the financing for your new small business : innovative solutions from the experts who do it every day / Sharon Fullen.
      p. cm.
  Includes index.
  ISBN-13: 978-0-910627-55-9
  1. Small business—Finance. 2. New business enterprises—Finance. I.
Title.
  HG4027.7.F85 2006
  658.15'224--dc22
                              2005033189

EDITOR: Jackie Ness • jackie_ness@charter.net

ART DIRECTION, FRONT COVER & INTERIOR DESIGN: Meg Buchner • megadesn@mchsi.com

BOOK PRODUCTION DESIGN: Laura Siitari of Siitari by Design • www.siitaribydesign.com

Printed in the United States

Here's What Industry Experts Say About
How to Get the Financing for Your New Small Business:

"Obtaining money for startup businesses can be challenging. This is a great guide for the new entrepreneur."

— N. Michael Phung, MBA, JD
Beltway Capital Inc., Custom Mortgage Solutions
www.beltwaycapital.net

"This book is extremely resourceful. It creates so many valid options that the business owner can feel empowered to make things happen... this book provides direct and simple solutions that enable today's small business owner to understand he can open doors he didn't even know existed."

— Howard Nevins, President
Marathon Financial Factoring Services
www.marathonline.com • 800-647-0850

"Sharon's book is a comprehensive look at owning a small business. From top to bottom, it covers all the bases that lead up to getting the capital to make a business become successful."

— Gary W. Honig, President
Creative Capital Associates, Inc.
www.ccassociates.com/blog

"The most crucial part of starting a business is the financing. Without money, many good business ideas will never make the transition from dream to reality. This book presents a balanced, unbiased overview of the many financing options available to today's entrepreneur."

— Steve Johnson, CEO
RealNvest, Inc.
www.FundYourDeal.com

FOREWORD

Walk down Main Street in any town in America and you'll be quickly reassured that America's entrepreneurial spirit is alive and well. According to the Small Business Administration, over 500,000 new businesses were formed during 2002—and if you're reading this book, you've probably either entered the pool or are wading in. You probably have a great idea for a unique product or service, tremendous energy, and a will to succeed. Unfortunately, the road to independence is littered with entrepreneurs with these traits.

Small, growing businesses face a variety of challenges. These challenges include, but are not limited to, finding the right employees, safeguarding propriety interests, developing market awareness, and operating at a profit. The relative importance of these issues is dependent upon the unique facts and circumstances of each business. However, one other challenge impacts almost every business: securing the financing necessary to execute the business plan. The reality is that even the most profitable businesses will, at some point, face working capital issues that will necessitate additional debt or equity financing. The good news is that there are an enormous number of financing alternatives for small businesses, from family loans to angel investors to public offerings. So how do you decide which source is right for you?

In this particular case, there is no substitute for research. Financing and structural decisions made by entrepreneurs at early stages can ultimately come back to haunt them. I have worked with many companies that sought venture capital early in their life cycle, only to be shocked when the businesses that they built were taken over by the new outsiders on their boards. Of course, there are numerous other examples where venture capital was critical to a company's ultimate success. These varying outcomes simply underscore the fact that it is never too soon to develop a business plan and consider your ultimate personal and professional goals. The right source of financing varies from business to business and will be driven by issues such as the relative importance of retaining control of the business, anticipated growth, volatility in sales and earnings, as well as your ultimate exit strategy.

How to Get the Financing for Your New Small Business: Innovative Solutions from the Experts Who Do It Every Day provides a comprehensive analysis of common—as well as uncommon—financing options available to small business owners. The book provides details on typical steps involved in connection with different sources of financing, as well as common pitfalls and issues. Additionally, it provides valuable insight into techniques you can use to more effectively market your business to potential lenders or investors, including techniques and resources for business plan development. Perhaps the greatest benefit is that the book creates awareness so entrepreneurs can make educated decisions early, to avoid unwanted surprises later.

Finally, there is a very fine line between success and failure, and success almost always involves a great deal of planning and hard work. The information provided in this book, combined with advice from legal and financial experts familiar with your unique circumstances, can help ensure that your plans and decisions are well thought out and that potential risks are identified and managed. So plan well and work hard, and hopefully you can become one of the millions of successful small businesses powering the American economy.

Christopher F. Meshginpoosh
Certified Public Accountant
Philadelphia, PA

Mr. Meshginpoosh currently serves as a partner in a Philadelphia-based accounting and advisory firm. Additionally, Mr. Meshginpoosh has served as a Senior Manager at a Big 4 firm, as well as an executive officer or board member of private and publicly held companies. He is licensed as a CPA in Pennsylvania and is a member of the Pennsylvania Institute of Certified Public Accountants and the American Institute of Certified Public Accountants.

TABLE OF CONTENTS

INTRODUCTION

CHAPTER 1 – LEARNING YOUR MONEY FORMULA

CHAPTER 2 – THE MONEY IS OUT THERE

CHAPTER 3 – YOUR BUSINESS PLAN

CHAPTER 4 – INVESTING IN YOUR OWN DREAM

CHAPTER 5 – NEITHER A BORROWER NOR A LENDER BE

CHAPTER 6 – YOUR LOAN PROPOSAL

CHAPTER 7 – VALUATION OF YOUR BUSINESS

CHAPTER 8 –
DEBT FINANCING VERSUS EQUITY FINANCING

CHAPTER 9 – UNCLE SAM HELPS OUT

CHAPTER 10 – GRANTS

CHAPTER 11 – VENTURE CAPITAL

CHAPTER 12 – INVESTOR ANGELS

CHAPTER 13 – INITIAL PUBLIC OFFERINGS

CHAPTER 14 – DIRECT PUBLIC OFFERINGS

CHAPTER 15 – STRATEGIC ALLIANCES

CHAPTER 16 – LEGAL CONSIDERATIONS

CHAPTER 17 – THE PITCH

CHAPTER 18 – GLOSSARY

CHAPTER 19 – RESOURCES

INTRODUCTION

You have to spend money to make money. Many entrepreneurs know this saying to be true, but what about the step before spending? After all, you have to have money to spend money. So how does a small business owner get the capital needed either to launch a new business venture or to grow his or her existing business?

This book will explore ways to underwrite your dreams, including how to select the right type of financing for your business and how to "sell" yourself, your company, and your ideas to the potential lenders and investors.

As a small businessperson, you play a vital role in our society. Your success is like a stone dropped in a pond — the ripples radiate well beyond the point of entry. Your success affects your family, your employees, your customers, your community, and even the U.S. economy. Our government, charitable organizations, and the business community have a stake in your success. So if you have a solid business idea and the ability to make it happen, others will want to invest in your dream.

DID YOU KNOW?

1. A small business is any independent business with 500 or fewer employees.

2. As of 2003, 5.7 million small businesses have at least one employee.

3. As of 2003, 17 million small businesses are sole proprietorships.

4. Fifty-three percent of small businesses are home-based.

5. Women own at least 50 percent of some 10.6 million firms.

6. The number of minority-owned firms is growing four times faster than all other U.S. firms.

7. Of all employers, 99.7 percent are small businesses.

8. Sixty to eighty percent of all new jobs (net) over the past ten years were created by small businesses.

9. Eighty-two percent of small businesses use some form of credit for financing.

10. Approximately 95 percent of new small businesses rely on personal financing (savings, second mortgages, and family or friend support).

MONEY, MONEY, MONEY

Angel investors invested an estimated $22.5 billion in 48,000 companies in 2004. Venture capital firms estimate that they invest between $3 and $5 billion annually. The Small Business

Administration (SBA) guarantees more than $10 billion in loans every year.

Borrowing wisely is important—even if it is from your own piggy bank. Initial financing may be a loan from Mom, but how you approach this business relationship and use the funds is just as important as borrowing from a bank. Chapter 2 will discuss the various types of personal financing and tips on how to make each work for you.

For the 5 percent of entrepreneurs who will rely on formal "outside" financing, remember that every new business starts with some type of personal financing. Investors and lenders expect you to be financially (besides physically and emotionally) invested in your dream.

Whether you need a few hundred dollars or thousands of dollars to launch your new business, there is money available to people with sound business skills and a solid business plan.

You have only one chance with a potential investor. You may only have ten minutes to tell your story, show your profit potential, "close the deal," and secure the money you need for your business.

CHAPTER 1

LEARNING YOUR MONEY FORMULA

If only it were this easy: Business Idea + Money = Success. Many businesses, large and small, have discovered they couldn't buy their way to the top. It takes more than an influx of cash to launch and grow a business.

There are few "do-overs" when it comes to seeking financing. You have only one chance with a potential investor. You may only have ten minutes to tell your story, show your profit potential, "close the deal," and secure the money you need for your business.

BE PREPARED

The most common mistakes made by beginning entrepreneurs result from a simple lack of preparation. All of the enthusiasm in the world cannot make up for a failure to research when seeking capital.

Before you fill out a loan application or contact a potential investor, you need to be prepared—in your head, in your heart, and on paper. A good place to start is with the creation of your "elevator pitch."

DEVELOP AN ELEVATOR PITCH

Imagine you were alone in an elevator with a rich investor. Here is your chance to pitch your idea. Can you capture his attention, sell him on your idea, and intrigue his entrepreneurial spirit before you reach the twenty-second floor?

Your elevator pitch, which should take about the length of an elevator ride to deliver, is a brief description that neatly sums up your business concept. It isn't a lifeless declaration—"I want to start a Chinese restaurant." It is a statement that captures the excitement and potential of your idea—"I'm starting a trendy restaurant featuring exquisite dinners from every region of China. I've hired a chef from a popular New York establishment, and renowned restaurant designer Barbara Lazaroff is working with us."

Your elevator pitch is also useful in helping you focus on your goals. You will find several ways to build upon your elevator pitch throughout the book.

KNOW YOUR INVESTORS

Both understanding the current market as well as anticipating and addressing the needs and concerns of typical investors are necessary when creating a business plan. Entrepreneurs need to show that their business will be capable of generating a steady flow of revenue with profits on the horizon.

Show that your team is competent and familiar with the target industry. Otherwise, to investors the risk may seem too great. Many investors rely on the "bet on the jockey, not on the horse" philosophy, or investing based on the person in charge.

FOCUS YOUR SEARCH

Focus your search on the sources most likely to deliver. Otherwise, you risk spending countless hours preparing deals that are destined never to materialize or to collapse at the last minute.

PLAN AHEAD

Predicting how long it will take to close a financing deal can be difficult, yet misjudging this can have devastating effects on your business. Planning ahead for secondary, or backup, financing can keep your business from stumbling.

If the time comes when the capital is needed and the deal still isn't closed, be prepared to have your prospects vanish. After all, customers are on a tight schedule too. The best time to raise money is *before* you need it, not *when* you need it.

BE FLEXIBLE

A good, solid business plan is a necessity, but entrepreneurs that are too attached to their plans tend to fail. There are several reasons for this:

1. The market is always changing. If a business cannot adapt to the market, it will struggle to create revenue. Any sign of stubbornness or inflexibility is sure to send investors running toward an investment headed up by someone who can deal with change.

2. Your assumptions are just that. As you set about creating a plan, you base statements and ideas on assumptions that may turn out to be inaccurate. Although a lot of

time and effort is put into creating projections, remember that they are only educated guesses of what sales will be like. If a business relies too much on its projections, and sales fall short of those projections, consequences can be disastrous.

3. Consumer demands and trends change. If a business spends too much time developing its product, by the time the product hits the market, the need for it may have passed or been filled by another vendor. You have to have a real product to have real customers, not a product in development.

REMEMBER TO MIND THE STORE

Sometimes, in an effort to help the business grow more quickly, entrepreneurs spend too much time searching for capital. Neglecting the day-to-day operations of the business can leave others with little reason to invest. If your business is not spending the money you've earned as effectively as possible, you might as well not be raising it.

BUILD A STRONG TEAM

Investors pay attention to your management team; it is the infrastructure of your company. Investors want to see that you have strong personnel resources. Investors know that it takes more than one person to make a company succeed. If potential investors don't have confidence in the team you've assembled, then they certainly won't have confidence in you.

WRITE A LEAN AND MEAN BUSINESS PLAN

Investors don't have time to read a business plan that resembles a novel. Try to keep it as short as possible without sacrificing essential information. Be concise when dealing with investors; they have no time to waste. Also, keep abridged versions or a synopsis of your plan handy in case an investor wants just the meat of it.

OWNERSHIP VERSUS CONTROL

Although a founder may have retained only a small percentage of the business ownership, he or she may retain a large percentage of the control of the business. It works the other way around as well. Investors can negotiate deals, especially with desperate businesses that have fallen on hard times in which they take over a substantial portion of the control without investing much capital.

STAY ON THE RIGHT SIDE OF THE LAW

No legitimate businessperson intends to break the law; however, taking shortcuts and being ignorant of laws regulating your business can derail even the most well-intentioned entrepreneur. Business law and regulations can be overwhelmingly complex and confusing. Unfortunately, ignorance of these laws does not absolve one from any wrongdoing.

Learn as much as you can about the laws in the following general areas:

1. **Employer-employee laws** — Liability, overtime regulations, and workplace safety.

2. **Protection of ideas**—Copyright laws, patents, and trade secret regulations.

3. **Contractual law**—What voids a contract.

4. **Securities**—Know the regulations that govern how you raise capital.

5. **Industry-specific government regulations**—Trade regulations, interstate commerce, and other local, state, or federal laws.

6. **Environmental laws**—Use of natural resources, pollution, waste, and ecological-impact laws.

Hire a Lawyer

Having an experienced corporate attorney is critical when starting a business. Although these specialists are expensive, they have experience in such key areas as employee negotiations, intellectual property rights, setting up stock-option plans, and state and federal tax laws.

Because legal errors can be costly, this is an investment that allows you to concentrate on other aspects of the business. Too many entrepreneurs believe that they don't need a lawyer. Competent legal counsel may not seem affordable, but ignorance can collapse your business.

Create Strong Agreements

When you write a contract, make sure your interests are protected, and leave yourself some options. Stay flexible, but be certain that all agreements are in writing and reviewed by your business attorney.

Keep Good Corporate Records

Keeping track of every meeting and transaction is essential to protecting the status of your company. Don't rely on anyone's memory or word. Poor recordkeeping can cause serious problems with the IRS. This, in turn, results in serious problems raising future capital.

Be sure to keep records of these commonly overlooked items:

1. Board meeting minutes

2. Shareholders' meeting minutes

3. Stock issuance

4. Stock transfers

Write Good Employee Policies

Poorly documented and unenforced employee policies are lawsuits waiting to happen. Although it is necessary to establish a good rapport with employees, don't let their standards fall below your own, putting your company at risk. Set clear policies and enforce them on Internet use, discrimination, sexual harassment, employee safety, and drug use. Your attorney can advise you on specific issues that your employee handbook must address.

Be sure that your employees understand that they are "at will" employees, meaning that you can terminate them at any moment (the other side of this is that they can quit at any moment) without your business being held liable.

Define Partnership Agreements

It may seem obvious that partners in a business must share the drive and will to succeed, but it is important to clearly define in writing what is expected of each partner.

The following points should be addressed in a partnership agreement:

1. The amount of capital each partner is expected to contribute.

2. A plan of action if the business needs more capital (where it's going to come from, are the partners expected to dig deeper into their own pockets, etc.).

3. A clear outline of each partner's responsibilities, workload, and time commitment to the business's operations.

4. A plan of action in case a partner dies or decides to leave the business.

Protect Yourself

When setting up a business, consider how at risk your personal assets will be. In many states, general partnerships hold the partners jointly liable for outstanding debts. This means that all of your personal assets are at risk if the business encounters a problem. Starting as a corporation or other limited liability entity can help you avoid liability issues.

Secure Your Intellectual Property

Intellectual property issues are as important in low-tech industries as they are in the worlds of software and computers.

Employees should always be required to sign confidentiality agreements. All company logos and trademarks should be registered, vital documents should be copyrighted, and, if applicable, products patented.

Protecting trade secrets is also important. The future of your business relies on it. Place copyright notices on all documentation, and have potential investors sign nondisclosure agreements when meeting with you. See Chapter 3 for additional information regarding nondisclosure agreements.

Resolve Conflicts Wisely

In the event of a legal dispute, leave litigation as the last resort. First attempt to resolve conflicts through mediation, arbitration, and settlement. Although settling may seem like giving up, it is often more cost effective and less time consuming than litigation. Because time and money are at the heart of any business, it is important not to be stubborn; standing on principle could hurt the business.

CAPITAL BUDGETING

Raising capital arbitrarily is no way to run a business. Before looking for capital, determine how much you actually need, working capital as well as capital for investments. The process of identifying and prioritizing the capital investments that increase the value of your business is known as capital budgeting. This process depends on restrictions and priorities.

Restrictions

Your choices are restricted because you can only raise so much capital and still service your debts and deliver investor returns.

You need to figure out exactly how much money is coming in and going out, and how much, if any, can be set aside for investments.

Priorities

Deciding which of your projects adds the most value to your business, and then ranking the projects accordingly, can help you evaluate where the money is going. Those projects that add the most value get more investment money.

At the heart of capital budgeting is the idea that a business will grow faster if it maintains a steady cash flow and invests in expansion in order to add sales to that cash flow. So, instead of paying off debt, the debt is paid down slowly in order to keep funds for expansion projects available.

Paying off debt over time will technically cost more in the long run, but only in terms of the debt itself. If the business uses its cash flow to expand, and sales increase, the amount of capital that is generated from that might outweigh the fact that servicing the debt requires monthly interest payments.

There are three primary methods for ranking projects and their value to the company:

1. **The Payback Method** — A simple method that ignores future possible cash outflows and does not use discounted cash flow (DCF) analysis. This method rates projects on how quickly they will be able to pay for themselves.

2. **The IRR Method** — Projects are ranked through this method by the investor's rate of return (IRR). This method takes into account cash flow structures by

measuring what is known as the hurdle rate, or the opportunity cost of investment capital, which is manifest as the appropriate interest rate, or rate of return.

3. **The Net Present Value Method** — Net present value (NPV) uses DCF analysis to rank projects by what they are currently worth to the company from an opportunity standpoint.

The IRR and NPV methods are used far more commonly than the payback method, simply because most businesses think in terms of cash flow. Without adequate cash flow, the owner of the business knows that the company is vulnerable to all sorts of unpleasant situations, including the inability to pay suppliers or falling behind in the industry because of lack of expansion.

At every level, our economy depends upon borrowing and investing. Even in a down economy, there is money available to start a new venture or to grow a healthy business.

CHAPTER

2

THE MONEY IS
OUT THERE

Lending money to businesses is the foundation of the banking industry. Venture capitalists do nothing but invest in people and ideas. At every level, our economy depends upon borrowing and investing. Even in a down economy, there is money available to start a new venture or to grow a healthy business. In fact, if your idea has merit and you can establish a plan, you may have better luck during slow investment periods. During economic booms, investors are bombarded with business opportunities — many of which, in hindsight, proved to be folly. When few dollars are available to invest, the marginal proposals are quickly dismissed.

SIX WAYS TO FINANCE A BUSINESS

1. **Give it** — The primary source for business financing is ownership contribution.

2. **Borrow it** — Commercial, government, or private loans range from micro small business seed money to multi-million dollar open lines of credit.

3. **Sell it** — Selling a part of your company to investors can provide needed capital, but sharing ownership has its drawbacks.

4. **Earn it** — Saving requires long-range planning and wise money management, but it is the most economical way to finance growth.

5. **Pledge it** — Private or public business development grants are available based upon your ability and willingness to "give back" to the community.

6. **Share it** — Find an upline sponsor (coach), employer, business, or individual who will subsidize your idea with the goal of enhancing their financial picture.

Money comes from four types of potential "investors," each with his or her own motivations:

1. **Owners** — You and your partners are motivated by dreams, desires, and needs. These can often cloud your decision-making abilities.

2. **Private parties** — Family and friends may be motivated primarily by friendship (profits are an added bonus) but it is serious when you enter into a business relationship.

3. **Commercial profit-making entities** — Banks, venture capitalists, and angel investors are primarily seeking profits (interest, ownership) and personal gain (bonuses, recognition, achievement).

4. **Nonprofit entities** — Government agencies and charitable foundations have missions to enhance lives and communities through economic growth and

development. They are motivated to "do good," but that doesn't mean they overlook good business practices.

BEFORE YOU SEARCH

Before beginning your money search, you must know what you need the money for, how much you need, what you can afford to "pay" for the money, and what you are willing to sacrifice for it. Chapter 8, "Debt Financing Versus Equity Financing," will help you make these determinations. Other helpful resources for developing a business plan can be found in Chapter 19, "Resources."

EXPLORING THE OPTIONS

Examining your business and discovering your entrepreneurial style are the first steps in finding the funding that matches your company's needs. When the need for money arises, entrepreneurs can become consumed by raising capital. Their judgment becomes clouded and their decision-making ability compromised. The cliché "the end justifies the means" is not always true. Your first step in exploring your financing options is to determine what you are willing to sacrifice.

WHAT WILL YOU DO TO FINANCE YOUR DREAM?

Here are a few exploratory questions to help determine your comfort level with various methods of acquiring startup or expansion financing.

1. Am I willing to make personal sacrifices? No new car, renting a less expensive apartment, eliminating your daily latte?

2. Can I emotionally handle the risk and debt incurred in starting a business?

3. Do I have a strong vision, and can I see myself as successful?

4. Am I willing to share the profits with a silent partner?

5. Will I resent paying a partner who doesn't work as hard as I do?

6. Is my idea (and future success) more important than my need to control the business?

7. Will I be able to tolerate "interfering" investors?

8. Am I open to unsolicited advice from investors?

9. Is my idea strong enough to support partners?

10. Can I afford the interest rate?

11. What are the risks in paying "too much" for a loan?

12. Will I have the ability to repay the debt on time?

13. Am I ignoring warning signals (about people, situations, and risk)?

14. Should I stop and regroup before proceeding?

15. Is my business plan ready to go?

AVAILABLE FINANCING SOURCES

The overview below outlines the types of financing available to businesses. Making the decision to start or expand a small business opens up a variety of considerations and options. Many burgeoning companies spend far too much time chasing down funds from sources that do not mesh with their business. Making the right deal with the right investors or lenders provides you with the opportunity to grow in a manageable and hospitable environment. Making the wrong deal with the wrong investors can cause serious problems down the road, setting you up for conflicts and even potential failure.

GIVE IT—YOUR PERSONAL INVESTMENT

Investors and lenders (except perhaps family and friends) will expect you (personally) or your business to provide a significant amount of the capital necessary to launch or expand your business. When an entrepreneur puts his or her own assets on the line, it sends the message that he or she is committed to making the company a success, thus making it easier to acquire supplemental funding from outside sources. (There are a few exceptions, such as seed money programs created to assist economically disadvantaged at-risk individuals.)

Investing Your Money

Nearly 80 percent of all entrepreneurs rely on personal savings to begin a new enterprise. Using personal savings also secures the entrepreneur's control and ownership of the business. Because it is your money, no debt is incurred and future profits aren't shared with investors.

Using personal assets is another way to fund a new business. Converting personal assets (furniture, equipment, and vehicles) to business use is the same as giving your business cash. Not only will you avoid purchasing these items, but you'll also be able to depreciate them. Check with your accountant on how to properly set up the conversion and depreciation schedules.

For many people, their greatest personal asset is their home. Lines of credit (using your home as collateral), refinancing, and home equity loans are often used. However, raising cash this way can be risky. In addition, personal credit cards, signature loans, and loans against insurance policies and retirement accounts are common ways of raising startup capital.

Home Equity Loans

Taking out a loan against your home to fund your business may seem like a viable source of capital, but the potential risk is significant. After all, your home is probably the most valuable thing you own, and gambling with it, especially on a startup venture, can be disastrous.

When deciding whether or not to undertake a home equity loan, you'll need to know how much equity you have in your home. For less than $500, an appraiser or local real estate agent can locate home sale comparisons for you to use as an estimate.

If you own your home outright, you can refinance without staking all of the equity you have in your home, leaving room for future refinancing should something go wrong. However, if you own 20 percent or less in equity, by no means should you ever consider borrowing against that. The funds you gain would be minimal, and the second lender would not hesitate to foreclose should trouble arise.

A good guideline is this: If you own more than half of the value of your home (meaning 50 percent or more as equity), then it is relatively safe to borrow against that equity, providing you are confident in your ability to repay the loan.

The best way to determine this is by following these steps:

1. Get your home appraised; if the value has gone up, you may own more equity than you think.

2. Figure out exactly how much you still owe on your mortgage (or mortgages).

3. Take the valuation delivered by the appraisal and subtract your debt to determine the amount of equity.

4. Figure your percentage by dividing your equity amount by the valuation amount. If it is less than 50 percent, you should probably find a different source of capital for your business.

5. If your equity is more than 50 percent, you may be in business. Now is the time to get some loan quotes.

6. Figure out how your business plan will be affected by this cash infusion, and make projections as to how long it will take for the loan to be paid off.

The most important thing, once the deal is done and you have borrowed against your home equity, is to service the debt effectively. Falling behind on payments can be disastrous, so make sure your business can handle it.

If possible, pay down the principal balance of the debt in order to get out of debt faster and regain the equity on your home.

Leveraging Your Credit

Leveraging your personal credit worthiness is another way to support your business. As a new business, you won't have any established credit. Your signed personal guarantee (based upon your personal credit history) can help you establish credit for your business. Be certain to ask your attorney about personal liability issues for all business debts. Protecting your personal credit and financial health is a key reason to incorporate.

When it comes time to attracting outside investors, a business that has already been active for a couple of years looks much more appealing than one just starting out. Starting small can be a wise decision. Your risk is minimized, your experience is earned, and you have a greater understanding of what you can do and what you need to do it!

BORROW IT—LOANS TO REPAY

Borrowing can save your business or act as a noose around your company's neck. When looking at various types of loans, consider such issues as collateral required, interest rates, and repayment terms.

Loans from Family and Friends

Asking for help from those closest to you can be another smart move when looking for capital. Since you already have a relationship with friends and family, there are no questions of trust, and a willingness to help already exists.

Interest-free or low-interest loans from relatives or friends can help a startup business gain important supplemental capital without having to take out a bank loan or give up control and profits to investors. You may even have an angel investor in the family.

Many people believe (and often rightfully so) that "going in business" with a friend or family member is not a good idea.

Approaching family and friends about borrowing startup capital should be done in a pressure-free, professional manner. Don't assume that they have to give you money or see the potential of your business idea. Cornering Aunt Tillie at a family dinner or your hitting up your dad on his birthday is rude. Remember, your personal relationship is more important than the money you might receive. (Read Chapter 5 for more information on borrowing from family and friends.)

Loans from Commercial Lenders

A bank loan is the most typical source of outside funding for most businesses. In fact, Small Business Administration (SBA) and state government loans are actually bank loans in which the government agency provides financial support and underwriting. (See Chapter 9 for information on government-backed business loans.)

Having a sound business proposal is the key element to obtaining a loan from a bank, credit union, or commercial lender. The lender will also factor in personal credit history, outstanding debt, and past business performance when reviewing a loan application for a new business.

Lines of Credit

A tempting source of short-term small borrowing for small businesses are micro loans. These alternative loans are often safer with lower interest rates. In addition, they can help fill the gap between expenditures incurred while manufacturing and delivering and the time it takes customers to pay in full. Lines of credit are also useful for making sure payroll is met.

SELL IT—SHARED OWNERSHIP

Investors are a type of owner, which means you must be willing to "sell" a portion of your business and future profits. Some investors are active participants in daily operations, while others offer guidance and support through board meetings. Still others prefer to let you do it all while they reap the rewards.

Family and Friends

Family members or friends can also be a great source of investment money. Unless your friend is a professional investor, you'll probably be able to negotiate a fair but less costly investment agreement. The trust factor works here as it does when borrowing money from family.

When considering these investors, ask yourself five questions:

1. Is this the type of person who panics about money after investing?

2. Does this person understand the risks and benefits?

3. Will this person want to take control or become a nuisance?

4. Would a failure ruin your relationship?

5. Does this person bring something to the table (besides cash) that can benefit my company and me?

Angel Investors

Angel investors are wealthy individuals (or small groups) who help launch small businesses by providing capital. These investors, who expect returns in seven years or so, look primarily for businesses they believe are going to fill a gap in the current market.

Angel investors tend to be successful entrepreneurs who want to stimulate unique business concepts and product ideas. Angels often specialize in investing in specific industries, so finding the right angel for your business is important. Remember that angel investors are experienced businesspeople who will notice if your business plan is filled with unrealistic projections and expectations.

Angel investors think long term and are willing to take risks beyond those of a traditional lender. Typically, they receive an equity share or partial ownership of the company in exchange for their funding. See Chapter 6 for more information on angel investors.

Venture Capital Firms

Like angels, these investor firms help small businesses expand by exchanging capital for equity or partial ownership. The primary difference between an angel investor and a venture capitalist is the source of the money — angels invest their own money while venture capitalists invest other people's money.

Venture capitalists follow more stringent investment guidelines and therefore are not as "emotionally" involved in your success. They want to invest significant funds (rarely less than $5 million) in high-growth industries. Frequently, they look to cash out in three to five years.

Venture capitalists also may play an active role in your company management, such as a board position. Expect these investors to have their own agenda that may or may not complement your business vision and direction. See Chapter 11 for more information on venture capital.

EARN IT—CREATIVE WAYS TO RAISE CASH

Some entrepreneurs have discovered nontraditional ways
to launch or expand a business. Networking with other
entrepreneurs and local established businesses is an excellent
way to find creative solutions to financing your company. Here
are some creative ways other entrepreneurs have used to earn
cash and discounts.

Saving

Trimming costs, as well as taking advantage of banking discounts
and rebates, and starting a business savings plan should have
first priority. Make regular deposits to start your future.

Bartering

The world's oldest economic system can be a great way to pay
for products and services your company needs. The Web has
made connecting with other interested parties much easier and
even introduced bartering programs in which a series of barters
can be set into play to earn bartering points.

Buying Groups

Maximize vendor/supplier discounts and reduce costs for
entrepreneurs needing everything from office supplies to raw
materials. Some are free; others require a membership fee.

Rebate Programs, Co-op
Marketing Funds, Support Freebies

These vendor-sponsored programs can be used to reduce your
inventory costs, pay for advertising expenses, train employees,

improve productivity, and decrease turnaround times.

Competitive Awards

Local, state, and national "contests" where companies compete for financial and support awards based on inventions, technological advances, excellent customer service, and hiring practices.

Employee Ownership Programs

Earn the money you need to launch a franchise. Domino's Pizza rose to the second largest pizza chain by assisting employees in owning their own franchise store.

PLEDGE IT— GOOD FOR YOU AND YOUR COMMUNITY

Contrary to what those infomercial "business advisors" may suggest, there aren't any pots of gold sitting around waiting for you. However, there are private organizations and public agencies that help businesses in exchange for their "giving back" to the community. Their helping hand can come in the form of one of the following:

1. Direct grants that require no financial repayment.

2. Repayable grants that are repaid from future revenues; zero repayment should your business fail.

3. Economic development programs that are designed to maximize your business's financial impact on the community.

4. Location grants that offer a financial incentive to locate

or move your business to provide economic stimulus to a community, city, or state.

5. "Soft" loans that offer less stringent qualifications and "softer" terms and conditions. These can be no-interest or low-interest loans.

6. Tax cuts, deferrals, and deductions that lower your business, personal, or property taxes.

7. Subsidies that pay for a portion of the cost of approved products or services. Your repayment is made by actively promoting your use of these goods/services.

8. Technology grants and support that transfers technology rights and sharing information that may be worth millions to a fledgling company.

9. Support in the form of free advice and access to resources that saves you consulting fees and improves your chances for success.

Your repayment could come in the form of locating in an economically depressed area, hiring special needs or high-risk employees, volunteering within your community, or mentoring others. The financial benefits for your company and your community can be substantial. In addition, being a good citizen never hurts your company's brand and community image.

SHARE IT—WIN-WIN SITUATIONS

Beyond every successful business is an assortment of people and companies that financially share your success. It's a simple concept—if you sell more hot dogs at your corner stand, the bakery that supplies the buns sells more too. Who in your personal or business life could benefit from your entrepreneurial success? Who might subsidize your idea in exchange?

FACTORING ACCOUNTS RECEIVABLE

Factoring companies exist to buy a small business's accounts receivables, immediately releasing anywhere from 50 to 80 percent of the value of those receivables directly to the business.

The remaining balance is relinquished once the receivables are collected, with the factor's help, and the factor takes 1 to 5 percent off the top. This is an expensive way to obtain cash, but can work effectively for businesses that do not qualify for any other forms of financing. Beware of missed repayment deadlines and escalating fees, both of which can keep you stuck in the factoring cycle for daily working capital.

OTHER FINANCING OPTIONS

If you think you have run out of financing options, think again. There are still many different financing options that may be right for your business. As with all the others, they require careful consideration.

Creatively raising capital is what running a business is all about. Very few businesses receive their capital from a single source, and those that do usually are not around for long.

The best approach to raising capital is a diverse set of funding sources, each tailored to a specific need of the business. Each type of funding has different benefits and drawbacks, as well as different turnaround times and amounts of paperwork.

Here are some alternatives to traditional sources of funding:

- Customer financing

- Purchase order financing

- Credit card financing

- Strategic alliances/mergers

- Leasing versus buying

- Employee stock ownership plans (ESOPs)

Weigh the positives and negatives before determining what alternative funding sources are right for your company. Taking the first source of capital that presents itself can be damaging to your company in the long run.

These funding sources are usually considered supplemental to traditional sources of financing. They are, however, important business practices that should be considered to keep your business in good financial shape. Having multiple sources of funding is by far the best way to finance a venture.

Customer Financing

Businesses recognize that they need one another to survive, and this recognition often leads to alliances and teamwork. When one business can help another, and in doing so, helps itself, it makes sense to form a good relationship.

This is the thought behind customer financing: If your business has a good relationship with one of your customers, particularly one with a lot of cash, then it is not unheard of to ask them for a loan, particularly if it is for something that will improve the quality of your services to them.

So here is the way it works: Perhaps your company needs a new piece of equipment, which will help you serve the needs of your largest customer. You then ask the customer for the money to buy the equipment, and in return, your company fills their orders for free, paying them with credit instead of cash.

This arrangement worked well for American Design, a Seattle ad-specialty manufacturer. They received $30,000 from one of their largest customers to buy a new embroidery machine, to be paid back with credit. According to the founder, the deal was fast and easy.

One thing to watch for, though, are the demands the lending company will place on your business. You must specify that they can only have so much product a month, or they might order more than you can produce, and without infusing any cash into the business.

A standard customer financing agreement has a minimum payback period of about six months, depending on the size of the loan. Make sure you specify a minimum payback period that your business can handle.

Purchase Order Financing

Some small banks will extend lines of credit to local companies with whom they have good relationships, based on that company's contracts or purchase orders. In other words, the bank lends the company the money that it expects to make, based on the incoming orders.

This type of financing is primarily used for solving issues of cash flow. Purchase order financing can help float a business through a busy season, enabling the business to maintain its inventory to generate higher sales.

This also allows the company to take on larger orders. The money that would ordinarily have come in after the fact is borrowed from a lender and used to help finance the order itself. This can help a business grow quickly, providing it stays current with its accounts receivables.

The financing rates on this type of credit line are often high, so entrepreneurs should exercise caution when entering into such an arrangement. When Chelsea Marketing and Sales began doing this in 1991, they eventually had to take out a second line of credit in order to pay for the first. They did, however, manage to retain all of their equity. This was their goal, until they could go public with the company. It was difficult and complicated, but it worked, and the company grew to more than $13 million in sales in a short period of time.

Credit Card Financing

When used carefully, credit cards can supply important supplemental or emergency cash flow. The "buy now, pay later" philosophy is one that can work well for businesses that might not have the capital needed to pay bills but expect it soon.

Many businesses will try to finance their entire operation using personal and business credit cards. Although this can work for brief periods of time, it is not recommended. The interest rates are high, and once you have reached your limit and you no longer have adequate cash flow, you could be out of business.

Moreover, using a personal credit card to fund a business is in direct violation of the consumer-cardholder agreement.

Nevertheless, thousands of companies do it, although it is still a breach of contract.

The best thing to do is to get a business credit card account. Once your business has established itself, you will begin to notice that credit card offers are coming in by the score, some with limits of as much as $100,000. This amount can be increased simply by maintaining more than one account. Inexplicably, banks that would never give a small business a loan for $100,000 will give the same small business a credit card with a limit in that same amount.

One argument, of course, is that the interest rates are much higher. This is obviously true. Interest rates for credit cards can be anywhere from 11 to 25 percent and higher. In addition, the rates are rarely fixed, and if you fall behind on payments, they rise immediately.

Still, these interest costs are often lower than the bank's loan fees. This has driven many businesses to use credit cards in lieu of bank loans, extending the time it takes to pay them off and saving money by swapping balances when another card with a better interest rate comes along.

Credit cards should be used primarily for fast capital that will be repaid in a short amount of time. The longer it takes you to pay off the existing balance, the more the money you borrowed costs you.

Take the case of Brents Sportswear, for instance. While attempting an expansion overseas in the fall of 1996, the company's cash flow began steadily diminishing. The founders, thinking this was temporary and that they would eventually pull through it, decided to use cash advances on their credit cards to make payroll. Although this did help them for a couple of months, soon their cards were maxed out to $150,000. When the company did not recover as the owners had hoped, they were unable to pay even the minimum on the balance. The founders' credit was not ruined completely, though, and soon after filing for bankruptcy, they were receiving pre-approved credit card offers, claiming that they could help rebuild the now-ailing credit.

On the other side of the coin is a West Coast manufacturer who has figured out how to use credit cards in an effective way. The founder got his suppliers to agree to charge his purchases the day after his card statement closed. Although typical billing cycles are 30 days, this founder was able to extend this period considerably by asking a small favor of his supplier. Because he spends nearly $1 million on that card every year, his Frequent Flier miles pay for all of his business travel.

So credit cards can work both ways for companies. When handled correctly, they can supply a great deal of emergency and short-term funding, sometimes less expensively and more easily than other sources of capital.

Used incorrectly, however, not only can the business suffer, but the founder's personal credit history also may be irreparably damaged.

To sum up, the good points of credit cards include:

- They are easy to obtain.

- Lines of credit can be as high as $100,000.

- They are accepted almost everywhere.

- The money is immediately available for emergencies.

- Incentive programs, such as Frequent Flier miles, can save money on other expenses.

- There is little paperwork and no extensive forms to complete.

The bad points include:

- The interest rates can be as high as 25 percent.

- Interest rates are not locked, and will rise considerably if you fail to make minimum monthly payments.

- Many cards have hidden fees, making them more expensive.

- Mismanagement of cards can ruin your personal credit.

- Having to make monthly payments on cards combined with other loans can cause huge cash flow problems for your business, forcing it into a cycle of debt.

Mergers/Strategic Alliances

Merging with a larger company can be wise if the business considering the merger feels choked by competition or wishes to shift gears and gain capital for a new venture. Many mergers, however, often lead to the founders of the small business either being bought out or being reduced to a minor decision-making role.

Mergers with similar-sized businesses may be a better decision. Combining resources and brain power along with complementary products, skills, and specialties to create a new partnership can be a solution for smaller businesses and increase their competitive advantage against major industry players.

A business in need of capital can ally with a larger business, supplier, or customer that has an interest in its technologies. Often some kind of value is exchanged. For instance, the larger company may demand exclusive rights to proprietary products, equipment, or ideas; a long-term purchasing agreement or set pricing from a supplier; specific distribution rights of products in certain locations; or special discount programs.

A strategic alliance can be a win-win situation. However, there are such risks as being bought out by a larger company, restricting future growth, damaging other business relationships, or potentially violating laws regarding free trade, price setting, or fair competition.

See Chapter 15, "Strategic Alliances," for more information.

Leasing Versus Buying

Leasing can work far better than buying with borrowed money for many small businesses. A major advantage to leasing equipment is that leasing allows you have up-to-date equipment, avoiding costly replacement as items grow obsolete. Also, leasing is usually less expensive than servicing a bank loan, allowing young businesses to conserve capital.

Businesses spend hundreds of billions of dollars a year leasing equipment. More than 80 percent of all businesses lease at least some portion of the equipment or property that they use.

A lease takes the form of a contract. Your business (the lessee) makes payments of a specific amount to the lessor over the course of the lease. How much is paid and how often are determined by the value of the equipment and its accompanying service agreement.

The two major areas of leasing for businesses are:

1. **Equipment leasing** in which businesses can lease everything from furniture to manufacturing equipment to fleets of vehicles.

2. **Real estate leasing** provides storage space, offices, retail space, parking, and warehouses. Also popular is the "sale and lease-back" method of real estate leasing, in which a company sells space to someone in order to gain capital, and then leases it back from them.

Differences in Lease Types

There are two primary lease types: The operating lease and the capital lease.

THE OPERATING LEASE

Operating leases require smaller monthly payments than standard bank loans. At the end of the lease term, the equipment or property is not fully paid for, leaving what is known as "residual value."

Once the lease term is complete, the lessee usually has the option of purchasing the equipment at the residual value, walking away, or renewing the lease based on the residual value. This purchase option is standard on an operating lease.

The lessor is responsible for all of the maintenance and service on the equipment. These service costs are factored into the monthly payments on the lease. Most, if not all, operating leases come with this kind of service contract. The lessee reserves the right to terminate the lease at any time, even before the end of the lease term.

THE CAPITAL LEASE

The payments on a capital lease are larger than those on an operating lease. This is because, usually, the equipment is paid off in full by the end of the lease term. The lessee does not receive any tax benefits, such as depreciation, associated with owning the equipment.

Capital lease payments are comparable to those of a standard term loan. This type of lease is far less common for businesses that wish to conserve cash by leasing instead of buying.

Deciding Whether to Lease or Buy

Although leasing does have its advantages, so does outright ownership. Whichever is going to be less expensive in the long run should not be the only factor in making the decision. Here are some additional items to consider:

Leasing:

- Smaller periodic payments

- Service contract

- Noncommittal

- Smaller down payment

- Option to buy

- Protects from owning obsolete equipment

- Increases company flexibility

- Helps cash flow

- More equipment can be obtained at once

- Preserves capital

- Improves credit

- Counts as an expense, not as a debt, so leverage stays low

Buying:

- Ownership

- Resale value

- Tax savings on depreciation and interest

- Usually less expensive in the long run

- No restrictions on use of equipment

- No penalties for termination of lease or misuse of equipment

Consider your company's leverage and how much debt it has assumed. Leasing helps keep leverage low by preventing you from having to borrow to purchase equipment.

Also, if you want your business to grow quickly, leasing will provide the opportunity to have more equipment available, which means the capacity to fill more orders, including large orders that other firms in your industry might not be able to handle.

One of the main reasons to lease instead of buy is to ensure your business is using up-to-date equipment. Technology is advancing at an unprecedented rate, and purchasing computers, for instance, can be a big mistake, as they might be obsolete before you have finished paying for them.

Employee Stock Ownership Plans

For mature businesses that have confidence in their cash flow and earnings potential, Employee Stock Ownership Plans (ESOPs) are a great way to provide internal funding. Employees become investors in the company, which improves morale and drive to succeed.

Once the ESOP is established, it borrows money from a bank or other financial institution (such as an insurance company) in order to buy stock from the company. The stock is usually purchased from the treasury or the owners and is used as collateral for the bank loan.

The business then uses the money from the sale of the stock for whatever purposes it needs. In exchange, it services the bank loan (principal and interest) through tax-deductible contributions to the ESOP.

The lender makes out well too, as half of the interest on the loan is tax deductible. The ESOP is very attractive to many businesses, because it can be a win-win-win situation: The lender gets a tax break, the company gets funding, and the employees get to invest.

Alternatives to a bank loan or business line of credit that may be suitable for interim needs and emergencies are discussed in more depth in Chapter 17.

CHAPTER

3

Your
Business Plan

N o financing search is successful without a business plan. Knowing what you want to do, how you'll accomplish it, and how much money you'll need to reach each stage of growth is critical—for yourself as well as for your investors and lenders. Even if 99.9 percent of your business financing comes from personal resources, it is essential that you create a financial plan with cash flow and profit projections to set goals and keep you on track. Nothing kills a business quicker than undercapitalization and financial surprises.

SOUNDING GREAT

An essential element in obtaining capital from outside sources is the ability to make your business sound great on paper. Even if your business runs very smoothly, your management team is top notch, and your products and ideas are high quality, you must communicate those things to an investor.

When communicating with potential investors, it is important to remain clear and honest. Investors and bankers alike often encounter entrepreneurs with big ideas and nothing to back those ideas up. By presenting your business in a professional manner, you are already one step ahead of the game. Nevertheless, do not rely on the content alone to convince people to give you money. Investors want to know they are dealing with someone who has his or her affairs in order

Although lenders and investors may seem a bit cold-hearted, their apprehensions when dealing with early-stage and startup ventures are quite valid; there is great inherent risk in staking cash on someone's untested idea.

As an entrepreneur, you must understand this risk and respect it. Do not expect investors and bankers to be as in love with your idea as you are. They've heard it all before, and chances are good that they've been through the misery of funding one or two failed ventures.

THE BUSINESS PLAN

A business plan serves as the mouthpiece for the business, expressing the company's goals, standards, and needs. It also helps keep the management team focused on specific aspects of the business. Revisiting the plan regularly helps you keep the broader picture in focus.

A business plan is a document in which you:

1. Describe your new or existing business.

2. Define your customers' needs and your ability to meet them.

3. Explore competitor strengths and weaknesses in order to outperform them.

4. Address possible stumbling blocks to success.

5. Establish yourself and your team as capable businesspeople.

6. Detail marketing strategies to capture market share.

7. Set benchmarks and goals for launching, developing, and profit making.

8. Provide financial projections and returns on investment.

9. Ask for money to support your success.

10. Tell investors and lenders "what's in it for them."

Business plans should sell your business to investors without endless financial projection spreadsheets or tedious descriptions of complicated technologies. An investor should be able to ascertain, at a glance, who you are, what you sell, who buys it, how you expect to grow, and what you plan to do in order to make that growth occur.

To create a successful business plan, define the business's goals and achievements. This is especially helpful when devising expansion strategies, launching product lines, or embarking on new ventures. Regularly updating the business plan makes it a powerful and practical decision-making tool.

WHO WILL NEED YOUR BUSINESS PLAN?

Investors (family, friends, and outside professionals) will need a complete version of your business plan to review its profit potential. Lenders (bank, credit union, government, family, and friends) will also need a complete version to determine your ability to repay loans. Both will look at your concept, along with your financial projections.

Potential investors and lenders will have their own agenda that affects what they want to see in your business plan. Family and friends should be able to see that their loan can be repaid.

Bankers should see that your business will have ample capital and resources for continual operation for several months (ideally for more than a year) and sufficient profits to repay your loan.

Investors should see that your business has excellent profit potential. They will look at the numbers first. A plan that doesn't demonstrate an ample return on investment may not be worth the time. Investors also want to see that you and your team have the ability to start and operate a successful business.

Philanthropic organizations should see that you, your community, and your business meets their criteria for economic support. They will consider your ability to repay your loan. If you are applying for a grant, they will look at your potential for success, contribution to the community (creating jobs, paying taxes, and rejuvenating neighborhoods), and need.

Government agencies should see that your business is capable of repaying loans. Grant applications will be reviewed for their ability to satisfy the grant program's mission.

CONFIDENTIALITY AND NONDISCLOSURE AGREEMENTS

The information you gather and report in your business plan is confidential. Although it may not be "top secret," it is wise to have interested parties sign a nondisclosure agreement before receiving your plan. A nondisclosure agreement outlines that the information is proprietary and confidential and not to be shared, copied, distributed, or discussed with unauthorized parties. This agreement should be in writing. Investors may be hesitant to sign a nondisclosure; however, terms can be negotiated. An attorney can assist you with an appropriate agreement for your situation and advise on when to use it.

Please note: Bankers, lenders, and venture capitalists are professionals bound to confidentiality. Requiring a nondisclosure agreement (or contract clause) may be considered insulting.

THE STRUCTURE OF THE PLAN

There are certain basic elements that should be contained in all business plans. This uniformity makes it easier for busy executives to scan and review the applicable sections quickly. Your plan will include:

1. The Executive Summary

2. Company Description

3. Product Overview

4. The Marketing Plan

5. The Management Team

6. Operations

7. Financial Projections

8. Appendices

A typical business plan should be between 20 and 40 pages long, not including the appendices or financial projections. However, you may only need six pages to tell your story. Be certain that all important decision-making information is described and supported by the facts, leaving out unnecessary puffery and statistics. Provide the facts necessary to determine the viability and worthiness (from a lender's or investor's point of view) of your business idea.

The Executive Summary

The most important section of any business plan is the executive summary. Think of the executive summary as the preview to a blockbuster film. The summary is a marketing tool designed to entice investors to learn more. Successful investors are bombarded with proposals, so you must grab their attention and sell them on the profit potential of your plan. Often investors dismiss the plan after reading the executive summary; however, if you have captured their interest, they will either read on or pass it to another reviewer for further investigation.

This document, while positioned first in the order of your plan, should be the last part written. The executive summary should contain only information that appears elsewhere in the document and should be between two and three pages in length. The summary presents the critical details of the plan (once it is completed) with a heavy emphasis on the size of the opportunity and any advantages your ideas will give you over your competitors.

Your Plan Outline

1. A brief description of the company.
   - Include the name of the company, the business of the company, and its history.

- Be clear about your objectives for the business.

- Other facts to include would be why you started the company, your mission statement, and your business model.

- The tone of the plan should be professional and enthusiastic.

2. The company's products and services:

   - Describe what the company makes or does in simple terms.

   - Avoid buzzwords and jargon if possible. If you can't, make sure everything is clearly defined.

   - Emphasize how your product or service makes the customer's life easier.

   - Describe future generations of the product or service already in development.

   - Include what needs to be accomplished in order to market your product or service.

3. Your industry and target market:

   - Present an accurate description of your industry and target market.

   - Don't exaggerate your market potential. A perceptive investor will notice exaggerations and take them as a sign of incompetence.

   - Realistically describe potential customers.

4. The competition:

- Identify the competition.

- Profile potential competitors fairly, accurately describing their weaknesses and strengths. Their successes may provide clues as to how your business might position itself.

- Think to the future and offer strategies for keeping the competition at bay.

5. Your marketing plan:

- Describe how you will reach your target market.

- Include what the media and industry analysts say about the current market atmosphere.

- Talk about how you will capture your share of the market. Be specific—discuss how you plan to strengthen the company's image and what measures will be taken to generate customers and leads.

6. Your management team:

- Give brief descriptions of the key members of your team and what they have accomplished together and in previous positions.

- Include whom the current ownership consists of and the structure of the team.

- Discuss possible new employees (or consultants) needed to complete or augment the team.

7. Previous or planned strategic alliances:

   - Alliances with other respected businesses or individuals can increase investor confidence.

8. Operations structure and existing or needed facilities:

   - To help the investor visualize the operation, provide physical descriptions of the space in which the product or service will be produced or rendered.

   - Include lists of your vendors and suppliers along with why you selected them.

9. Admit the risks involved:

   - Be honest about risk factors. Awareness of the risks of doing business is one sign of a mature entrepreneur. Investors will look at this closely.

   - Outline how you will plan to deal with inevitable market changes that could affect your business.

10. Capital needs and investor returns:

    - Describe in detail how much capital your business needs as well as your time frame.

    - Detail anticipated repayment or profit-sharing timetables. Investors want to know how quickly they can see a return.

11. Financial projections:

    After an investor decides to look seriously at a business plan, he or she will carefully review your financial projections. Every financial detail of your business is not needed, but be able to back up everything presented.

- Prepare profit-and-loss projections for the next five years.

- Provide monthly breakdowns for the first two years.

- Outline annual breakdowns for the past three years.

- Include predictions of your cash flow cycles.

- Describe investor exit-strategy details.

- Discuss possible future financing needs.

12. Appendices:

- Other nonessential items to substantiate your business concept.

- Articles of interest — industry analysis, economic indicators, competitive reviews.

- Advertisement samples — marketing and branding materials.

- Customer testimonials or investor references.

- Product photographs or renderings.

It is important that the entire team be involved when writing the plan. Otherwise, the plan may focus too heavily on one aspect and ignore others. The plan should be well-balanced and concise, supported with hard data.

WHO SHOULD WRITE MY PLAN

The person who gains the most wisdom from the research and writing of the business plan is you. By writing the plan yourself (or with the help of business partners or key employees), you will be able to document your ideas, ensure that the research is appropriate and accurate, and gain a better understanding of the financial aspects of operating your business. Your plan should incorporate your dreams and passions—no one else is better suited to that task.

If you simply cannot see yourself writing your own plan, there are business plan writers who, for a fee, will do all the dirty work. Here's what you should look for in a well-qualified business plan writer:

1. **Writing experience**—Review business plan samples along with other business writing. It takes a specific talent to be able to write insightful and compelling business documents. Remember, your plan must function as a sales piece to sell your idea; as a plan of action, and as a set of realistic and attainable goals.

2. **Research experience**—Facts and analysis are required to support your ideas. Can your business plan writer handle a portion of this for you? Does he or she know what types of research are needed to create a customized plan?

3. **Listening abilities**—Your plan is a reflection of your dreams and desires. Never hire someone who doesn't listen carefully to what you have to say.

4. **Questions**—Does the writer ask a lot of in-depth questions or want you to fill out a short form? The more

the writer knows about you, your business proposal, and your concept, the better the finished plan will be.

5. **A business background** — Does the writer have a business background that will provide an understanding of what it takes to be a successful businessperson? Business training can be a plus.

6. **Strong references** — Word-of-mouth is the best way to find any service provider. Ask other businesspeople for a referral. If that isn't possible, ask for a list of references that you can contact personally.

WHAT IT WILL COST YOU

Paying for a comprehensive plan can be costly. Pricing may be based upon the research required, length of plan, turnaround time, and financial reports to be generated. A custom plan will have a custom price; expect to pay between $1,200 and $10,000 for a top-notch, professional business plan. Pricing variables are also based on your intended use, local prevailing rates, and the expertise of the plan writer.

Be aware that it takes time to develop a professional business plan, and time is money. Plans that cost substantially less will be boilerplate projects that cover just the basics. Outside investors and lenders see these often and won't give you any bonus points for this type of plan.

Expect more personalized service and some advice. Review what is included with any quote along with any built-in review and revision procedures. Once you sign off and accept your plan, additional work will mean additional costs.

Most writers will require a deposit, periodic payments (for projects running longer than a month), and the balance upon completion.

SEARCHING FOR A BUSINESS PLAN WRITER

Before you begin the search process, you must be able to tell potential candidates what you want, when you want it, and what data and information you can give them. Writers may actually interview you. Others will have complex forms that you'll complete. The better prepared you are, the better results you'll get.

Tell Them What You Need

When interviewing potential business plan writers (also known as business plan consultants), the first thing you should do is clarify who does what. Will you have to provide them with all background research on customers, competitors, economic situations, and financial reports? Can the consultant provide you with secondary research? If the writer isn't local, who will gather community-specific information? Does the writer have experience in your industry? Save time and money by doing some basic research before asking for bids or proposals.

Tell Them What You Want

Write down specifics. Create a list of purposes and who will be reviewing your finished plan. Develop your elevator pitch describing your future or current business. Don't be afraid to share your passion. If prospective plan writers are bored with the facts, they may never "catch the spirit." A business plan is a business document, but it is also a sales piece.

Tell Them When You Need It

Writers will need to have an approximate completion date to provide you with a quote. If your time frame is flexible, you won't pay any "rush" charges. However, don't let it drag on or you'll lose your momentum and frustrate your consultant.

Tell Them What Resources You Have

Will you provide all the supporting data? Do you have research already completed? Do you have an accountant who will help with the financials? Is there an attorney to advise and review your business structure? Do you have a business plan that you have used in the past? What else can you provide the writer so they can deliver what you want and need?

WRITE AN RFP

In choosing a business plan writer, you must be able to tell each prospective consultant your requirements. The more specific you can be, the more accurate the quotes will be. A good way to accomplish that is with a written Request for Proposal (also known as an RFP).

An RFP describes the task (service or product) to be provided, outlines the scope of the need, establishes what qualifications are required, and asks consultants to bid. Having a set of "rules" from which to work will help consultants give you an accurate quote. In addition, you'll know that each bid is based upon the same criteria so you don't have to factor in variables when comparing pricing and services to be provided.

If I Could Only Write an RFP

RFPs can be report-like; however, a basic outline clearly defining your needs and expectations can be quite adequate for quoting purposes. Quotes will be based upon your specifications, so provide as much information as possible, be accurate, and have a clear set of expectations. You'll need a brief RFP if you want to search for business plan writers through various consultant and business service Web sites, such as Guru (**www.guru.com**) or Elance (**www.elance.com**). Many of these sites are free to businesses seeking assistance.

CONTRACTS AND AGREEMENTS

Your business plan writer should have a standard consulting contract that you will need to read carefully. This should be reviewed by your attorney before signing. The contract should be a "work for hire" agreement in which you own all copyrights to the complete plan, including all original research, artwork, diagrams, and charts. The contract should also prevent the writer from using your name or any part of your plan for advertising or marketing purposes without your written permission. You may also want to include a nondisclosure agreement.

The contract will also outline periodic payments and what constitutes "completed and accepted." Watch for errors and omissions, and don't sign off on anything that isn't correct to the best of your knowledge.

HELP! I'M WRITING MY OWN BUSINESS PLAN

The analysis skills used in developing your business plan are the same skills you'll use to become a successful business owner. Now is the time to learn all about your community and competitors, practice reading and interpreting financial reports, calculate your break-even numbers, and create a real-world, I-can-be-successful-with-this budget. Once you aggressively begin your launch, you'll need to make quick decisions based upon solid research. When your doors open, having this information will improve your ability to handle the financial challenges that are inevitable in any business.

If you are hesitant about your own research and writing skills, there are plenty of resources to guide you, along with experts to review and fine-tune your finished plan. There are books, software programs, support consultants, classes, and seminars designed to help you with the gathering and writing process.

WEB-BASED ADVICE

The Web is brimming with information on writing business plans. Several Web addresses are listed in Chapter 19, "Resources."

BUSINESS PLAN CLASSES

Classes or seminars are available online, via the telephone, at the local community college, or through your state's small business or economic development agency. Business plan writing classes for entrepreneurs are an excellent time and money investment. You will not only learn the standard format (what your plan must address), but you will also be taught other helpful skills. In addition, you will have the opportunity to network with peers. Classes often feature local experts (bankers, accountants, lawyers) who also offer one-on-one counseling.

Find business plan writing classes and seminars by contacting:

1. SCORE (**www.score.org**) for local classes.

2. NxLevel (**www.nxlevel.org**) for local nonprofit programs and classes.

3. Community college or university's school of business.

4. Chamber of commerce or state small business development agency.

5. Local economic development nonprofit organizations.

6. Business banker or accountant.

7. State and/or national trade associations.

8. Local newspapers (and their Web sites) and business journals.

To find a class on the Web, consult these sources:

1. Writing Trainers (**www.writingtrainers.com**)

2. Web Campus (**www.webcampus.stevens.edu**)

3. Small Biz Lending and SBA slideshow class (**www.smallbizlending.com/resources/workshop/ sba.htm**)

To participate in a teleclass training, you will be asked to call a specific phone number and input an assigned code. You will then be connected with the lecturer and other attendees. Typically, you'll have to pay any long-distance fees in addition to the tuition. Here are a few available sources:

1. Rebel Business (**www.rebelbusiness.com**)

2. Career Masters Institute
   (**www.cminstitute.com/EntreprenurialEagles.html**)

3. Parker Associates
   (**www.asparker.com/freecoaching.html**)

4. Write Your Own Pink Slip
   (**www.writeyourownpinkslip.com**)

SEMINAR WORKSHOPS

For seminars on business plan writing, contact:

- Quantum Business Solutions (**www.qbizsolutions.net**)

- SCORE (**www.score56.org/seminars_workshops.html**)

SOFTWARE-SPECIFIC CLASSES

When reviewing and choosing business plan software, consult online tutorials and/or third-party consultants to guide you with specific business plan software packages. These classes should not be for software technical support; rather, for how to write your plan using the tools provided.

BOOKS

Atlantic Publishing has recently published *How to Write a Great Business Plan for Your Small Business in 60 Minutes or Less* with a companion CD. To order, call 1-800-814-1132 or visit **www .atlantic-pub.com**. Additional resource books can be found in Chapter 19.

BUSINESS PLAN SOFTWARE

Technically all you need is a word processor, a calculator, and a printer to produce a professional business plan. However, not everyone feels comfortable with the process, and that is where business plan software can be helpful.

The interactive nature of business planning software guides you through the entire process, making it a wise investment. Software templates with a fill-in-the-blank format and sample business plans can stimulate ideas and help you overcome a frightening "blank page."

Too Good to Be True

No matter what software packages or Web programs promise:

- A solid, well-researched business plan cannot be written in one day.

- A software manufacturer cannot guarantee financing.

- Basic knowledge of accounting practices and financial reporting is necessary.

- Never use the canned text provided. Review the examples, and use your own words based upon your own beliefs and research.

Try Before You Buy

With Internet access, you can view demos online and download trial versions. Most trial versions have all the features available to test except for the functions of saving and printing. Some software developers offer industry-specific templates and sample plans. Review these for appropriateness. However, software that is not industry-specific can still be helpful.

ACCOUNTING SOFTWARE

QuickBooks Premiere 2003 and up (Intuit®, **www.quickbooks. intuit.com**) has built-in financial-planning capabilities including a Business Planner function using Ultimate Business Planner (see page 81).

Intuit's Quicken Home and Business versions offer some limited financial projection capabilities. Their "business planning" interactive link refers you to Palo Alto Software, makers of Business Plan Pro (see details on page 79). Microsoft Money Small Business Edition also has some basic financial-planning capabilities.

WORD PROCESSING SOFTWARE

Word processors offer outline capabilities and other document writing features. Business plan templates are available free from Microsoft at **http://office.microsoft.com/templates**. If you are an experienced word processor and spreadsheet user, you may find that these two are all you need. If you own WordPerfect or another full-featured word processor, check the template folder and their Web site for additional resources.

SPREADSHEET SOFTWARE

Excel (part of the Microsoft Office Suite) and other spreadsheet programs now come with a variety of financial and accounting templates. Additional templates including break-even analysis and startup costs for Microsoft products are available at the Microsoft Web site. Lotus 1-2-3 and other full-featured spreadsheets offer similar sales projection and financial-reporting templates.

PRESENTATION SOFTWARE

You may want to include an electronic presentation and graphics in your business plan. PowerPoint (found in the Microsoft Office Suite) can be a useful tool. Free templates can be found at the same Microsoft address.

MORE FREE TEMPLATES

Below are a few resources for free business plan templates. Remember the adage: you get what you pay for. All work with the Microsoft Office line.

- Money Hunter (**www.moneyhunter.com**) — free downloadable Word template.

- Bank of Canada (**www.bdc.ca/en/business_tools/ business_plan**) — free English and French versions.

- VFinance (**www.vfinance.com**) — free downloadable template.

- Free Webs (**www.freewebs.com/business_plans**)

- VCAonline (**www.vcaonline.com/resources/bizplan/ freetemplate.asp**)

- SCORE (**www.score.org/template_gallery.html**) — free templates.

BUSINESS PLAN-SPECIFIC SOFTWARE

There are two basic versions of business planning software: stand-alone and template-based.

Stand-alone software is a complete package and requires only a computer and printer. Template-based (also known as add-on software) are forms and guides to be viewed and used within common word processing and spreadsheet programs.

- **So which should I choose?** The answer is the one you believe you will be most comfortable using. However, you'll have more choices if you select a stand-alone version.

- **Should I spend more on software to get a "better plan"?** The true value of your plan is what you put into it. The professional packages available from leading software manufactures are developed by marketing and executive experts. These software packages are lifeless guides until you put your personality and enthusiasm into them.

- **I need help with my financial section.** Some packages provide extensive financial reporting capabilities. Industry-specific financial formulas and ratios are available on some packages. Preformatted spreadsheets or financial calculators will increase the cost of the software package, but if you will be handling the projections by yourself, the investment is worth it.

One of the best ways to select a business plan software package is a personal recommendation. Ask your family, friends, and other business owners (including your accountant) for their experiences. Even if you get an "old review," significant software changes or enhancements are rare, except for Web-based plan writing and the support resources available on the manufacturer's Web site.

Stand-Alone Products

Business Plan Pro (Palo Alto Software, **www.paloalto.com**), introduced in 1995, is a top seller. This package has a standard edition retailing at $99 and a premier edition at $199.

- The premier edition allows you to collaborate with others and offers additional financial spreadsheets and analysis tools.

- An online Flash demo (requires Macromedia's Flash Web browser plug-in) is available online along with a few sample plans. No downloadable trial version is available.

- Works with Windows 98 and later, and requires 100MB of hard disk space. No Mac version. Requires Internet access for some features.

- Can import Intuit QuickBooks and Microsoft Excel data; however, does not require either program. Must cut and paste to insert word processing text.

- Available in English, Spanish, and Portuguese, and for United Kingdom and Canadian users.

- Up to four free technical support incidents (toll call, fax, e-mail) and $10 per call thereafter.

- Available at company site, office supply and software retailers, and major online bookstores.

Business Plan Writer Deluxe (Nova Development, **www.novadevelopment.com**) is priced competitively with Business Plan Pro's standard edition. A free trial can be downloaded from their site after providing them with basic contact information.

- A PlanAudit™ feature checks your plan for spelling accuracy and math errors.

- Audio and video help included, along with sample plans and case studies.

- Provides help on forecasting and financial reporting with color charts.

- A 10,000-piece collection of business graphic clipart is included; however, this isn't typically of any significant value.

- Kiplinger's Business Attorney software with legal forms is included. Requires Windows 98 and later. No Mac version.

- Can import QuickBooks® Pro data and export to Word and Excel.

- Can create PDF files.

- Multi-user collaboration requires Internet access and their Plan Write Central membership (no pricing shown on company Web site).

- Free technical support via email or toll call.

- Available at company site, office supply and software retailers, and major online bookstores.

Ultimate Business Planner (Atlas Business Solutions, Inc., **www.bptools.com**) uses the question-and-answer format with explanations of terms. Powers QuickBooks Premier Business Planner; full version of this planner included in Intuit QuickBooks Premiere 2003 and later.

- Works with Windows 98 and later. No Mac version. Requires 16MB of free hard disk space.

- Includes an online demo slideshow; 90-day unconditional money-back guarantee.

- Thirty-day free technical support to toll number or via e-mail. Priced at $99 retail; it can be downloaded immediately from the company Web site or you can order a CD.

Plan Write (Business Resource Software, **www.brs-inc.com**) offers three versions of plan software.

- Plan Write for Loans ($49.95) offers little customization, no sample business plans, and two free technical support calls.

- Plan Write for Business ($119.95) is a full-fledged plan developer suitable for most business needs.

- Plan Write Expert Edition ($219.95) adds expert review and analysis of your finished plan.

- Their MBA Wizard™ is designed to "learn" and provide advice based upon your specific data. The Business and Expert editions come with unlimited free technical support.

- Sixty-day money-back guarantee.

- Works with Windows 95 and later. No Mac version.

- Exports to Microsoft Word, Excel, HTML, PDF, and Rich Text Format (.rft).

Template Products

Two important advantages for template-style business planning products are that they don't require you to learn anything new and that they work with older Windows operating systems and Office packages.

Business Plan Builder (Jian, **www.jian.com**) requires Microsoft's Word and Excel. Can forward plan through software to Kinko's for printing and binding. Sixty-day guarantee. Works with Windows 98 and later, Microsoft Office 97 and later. 24MB of free hard disk space. Limited version available for Mac users.

OfficeReady Business Plans (Template Zone, **www.templatezone.com/business-plan**) are templates for Microsoft Office 97 and later. Templates are preformatted for Word, Excel, and PowerPoint with additional graphic support and advice. Works with Windows 95 and later.

Business Plan Template (Business Plan Success, **www.business-plan-success.com**) again these are templates that work for Microsoft Office 97 and later. Immediate download along with a variety of support guides. Works with Windows 95 and later.

For Mac Users

Mac users don't have much to choose from when it comes to programs written for the Apple operating system. Business Plan Builder offers a less expensive, scaled-down version for Mac users. A few manufacturers suggest using Microsoft's Virtual PC software to read Windows versions on your Mac; however, this is a costly solution. You are better off relying on your Mac word processor and spreadsheet. Any template that states that it will work with Microsoft Word or Excel should work with Office for Mac.

ONLINE PLANNING

Web-based business plan development services offer true fill-in-the-blanks convenience. Via secure password-protected login, you write your plan online. This may be a practical option when you need shared-user access. However, writing online isn't as convenient as it might seem. Remember to save your work-in-progress plan at every offered option.

Review site policies carefully, including security and privacy policies. Many online business-planning services have a less-than-professional appearance and their pricing indicates that they do not have the same value as the major software developers.

- **The Entrepreneur's Center (www.thebeehive.org/ ecenter/start/bizplan/business-plan-why.asp)** is one example of free online business planning.

- **Budget 21 (www.budget21.com)** offers a free trial to their online planning services and full-year access for $39.95.

- **PlanWare (www.planware.org/freeware.htm)** offers some free online strategic planning features.

- **Fundable Plans (www.fundableplans.com)** charges $39.95 to create your plan via the Web.

CHECK WITH A TRADE ASSOCIATION

Check with your state and national trade associations for member discounts on planning software. Online industry forums can also be a great place for recommendations.

STILL DON'T KNOW WHAT TO BUY?

Find Accounting Software (www.findaccountingsoftware. com) is a free Web-based service that is based on a few classifying questions (including a 10 to 15 minute telephone interview) will help you select business management and planning software.

For a full review of several business plan software packages, visit Home Office Reports at **www.homeofficereports.com**.

"BLANK SCREEN, GO AWAY"

Writing doesn't come easy for many people. Some would-be writers are intimidated by a blank piece of paper or computer monitor. Some guidelines to help you get started:

- Start with the easier parts first. Work on sections in any order you like.

- Write in longhand. The act of changing to a different medium can sometimes help. Not everyone feels comfortable at the keyboard. Write the entire document by hand, and have a typist or consultant format everything for publication.

- Write in a natural voice. Although the language of business can be stiff and formal, this shouldn't become an obstacle. Express your ideas and provide convincing arguments, then hire a business plan writer or consultant to create a formal business plan.

- Write what pops into your head. The first idea is often the best one. Write it down and then think about how you can edit or improve it. Ideas cannot vanish into thin air once written down.

COPING WITH WRITER'S ANXIETY

Sometimes writer's block (difficulty putting words on paper) turns into writer's anxiety. Purdue University offers some great tips for coping with the natural anxiety people feel when writing an important paper at **http://owl.english.purdue.edu/handouts/general/gl_anxiety.html**.

ERROR-FREE WRITING

- Remove all the extra words. A common mistake in business writing is to add unnecessary words. If in doubt, leave it out. Read the sentence aloud; if thought is clear, you don't need it.

- Don't rely on the software. Read and re-read your plan out loud. Have someone else review your spelling, grammar, and syntax.

- Set the document style for word usage and grammar to "formal," in which, for example, contractions are not used.

DOES YOUR PLAN...

1. Tell the story of your vision in a clear, concise manner backed by facts?

    - Include your dreams, but don't rely on superlatives and opinions that cannot be supported.

    - Remember, every business says it is the best, quality is excellent, and service is unequalled. Include ways to demonstrate those beliefs.

2. Describe a marketable idea based upon your dreams and supported with facts?

    - Provide proof that customers want your products or services and are willing to buy them at a profitable price.

3. Promote a few solid products or services?

    - Focus on starting small and growing – doing too much too fast can drain you financially, physically, and emotionally, setting the stage for failure.

    - Become an expert on your products or services, and allow yourself time to develop a healthy business before expanding.

4. Explain long-term benefits?

    - Promote additional benefits, such as environmentally friendly packaging.

    - Address negative issues, such as safe disposal, antidotes, secure packaging, and restricted purchase.

- Identify the elimination of potential risks or harmful aspects through the use of childproof, biodegradable, or recyclable packaging, for instance.

5. Describe strategies and goals for launching and developing your business?

   - Define your ideas; create practical strategies, achievable goals, realistic deadlines, and benchmarks for success.

   - Discuss your preparedness for dealing with unexpected issues.

6. Detail a clearly defined target market of size and buying power?

   - Identify your customers and why they are your ideal customers.

   - Develop a target market large enough to allow for continued growth.

7. Talk about your competitive advantage?

   - Explain how you plan to outperform your competition and develop your own unique brand identity.

   - Identify competitors' weaknesses.

8. Include managers, key personnel, and support staff with the skills and experience to make your business a success?

9. Outline your ability to control the quality and ability to deliver your products?

    - Discuss how you plan to supply your orders.

    - If you depend on an outside vendor or manufacturer for raw materials or wholesale products, explain how you will be able to maintain consistent quality and recover should they fail as a supplier.

10. Show realistic financial projections and include best-case, most likely, and worst-case scenarios?

    - Base your business on solid expectations, not "what ifs."

    - Best-case scenarios can be achieved, but focus on the most likely scenario.

    - Approach worst-case scenarios reasonably, identifying ways to overcome unexpected setbacks.

11. Demonstrate profitability in a relatively short period?

    - Identify when you expect to begin making a profit.

    - Explain how your business will be able to provide a large enough return to attract investors.

12. Show that you have made a personal investment?

    - A plan supported only by ideas and sweat equity (unpaid time you personally devote) is considered to be high risk.

PRESENTATION OF THE PLAN

It is important to make your plan as attractive and professional looking as possible. Although you don't want to seem incompetent, you also want to stand out from the crowd. For a professional presentation, remember the following:

- Select an attractive, conservative cover.

- Clearly list your contact information on the front cover.

- Choose a large, easy-to-read font.

- Number the pages. This seems obvious, but obvious things are often overlooked.

- Keep the plan current, and indicate a "last-revised date" on the front or inside cover.

- Document your sources.

- Keep track of who has copies of your plan, making sure they are returned.

- Include a confidentiality statement in the document, but do not expect an investor to sign a nondisclosure agreement.

- Include important names in the document, being certain that the person whose name you are dropping actually knows who you are.

- Be concise.

As the founder of the business, know your business plan backward and forward. Nothing looks less professional than someone shuffling through his or her own business plan scrambling to find a piece of information. If you don't know the information off the top of your head, you should know exactly where it is located inside your plan.

By projecting your cash flow and working capital needs, you will have a better understanding of how much money will be coming through the door every day to pay vendors, lenders, and employees. Before investing your entire nest egg or borrowing more money, decide if you have enough money to keep you afloat until the business is profitable. Insufficient capital is a primary reason new businesses fail.

WRITING TIPS

Although this chapter may not provide you with the in-depth plan-writing information you need, these guidelines and resources can start you on the right path.

- Determine your business viability before approaching lenders and investors.

- Have an outside adviser review your plan. Find other people in your community who can provide you with advice, recommendations, and a critique of your plan. Your local university or community college may have a business development adviser on staff.

- Include employees when creating your plan. Employees are powerful resources — tap into their expertise. Your plan will improve and your employees will feel valued.

- Emphasize your personnel resources. Investors look for

more than a marketable idea; they want to build upon the strengths of people.

- Create a believable mission statement.

Mission Statement

Also known as a statement of purpose, your mission statement is similar to the objective section of a résumé. This statement should capture the reasons why you personally want to be in business, what you want to accomplish with your business, who your business serves, and what your company is (or will be).

Typically, a mission statements is less slick than an advertisement and more personal than a sales pitch.

- Think about what you want customers to receive from your company.

- Keep it as short as possible; never more than three or four sentences.

- Write clearly and concisely.

- Be straightforward and realistic.

- Look at sample statements of purpose for creative stimulus, but don't take one as your own as it simply won't capture the essence of your plan's message.

- Read *Creating Mission Statements for Smaller Groups* by Beverly Goldberg ($3.95 PDF download at Amazon.com).

- Write a product or service list. Lists are a great way to put ideas on paper. Lists can be a single word or an entire thought to explain the topic. Ideas for lists include:

— To help you develop your niche—what you do best and promote most—create another list that answers the question, "What makes your products and/or services unique or special?"

— How do you differ from your competitors? Are you higher priced? Open longer? Write down every difference.

— What special resources do you have going for you? This can be anything from name recognition within your community to outstanding chef awards to a patent or trademark.

— How will you produce your product/service? Will everything be made in-house? What special equipment will be required?

— Are there any obstacles or negatives associated with your products? Will you need to rely on hard-to-locate items? Are there limited vendors capable of supplying you?

— What products/services are in your future? Will you be able to respond to trends? Will your customers want you to?

• Conduct feasibility studies and explore different marketing, financial, and operational scenarios. A feasibility study/analysis compares the various "what ifs" and weighs the pros and cons. This helps in decision making and problem avoidance.

— Your feasibility analysis should tell readers in strong words what your study proves. Two or three concise paragraphs are plenty. Below is an example of integrating a study's results.

— Many business plan writers or consultants can provide feasibility services.

— Review the feasibility analysis spreadsheets in your business plan writing software.

— Refer to your financial studies as proof that your plan is feasible.

- Such sentences as, "In year two, the restaurant will have recouped its initial startup investment as illustrated in Report 4B" or "Based on the current dining trends and our increased customer capacity, we will have ample sales volume and profits to cover all outstanding loans and payables within the 36-month loan period. See Report 4 on page 22."

- If your business plan is solid and you have established an ability to repay a loan or give an investor a reasonable return on their investment, tell your readers. If you are asking for loans or investments, discuss how this will positively affect your outcome. "The additional capital will allow us to expand our current facilities by 100 percent. Based upon our historical product life cycles, the repayment period would be less than the ten-year length of the loan."

- Don't underestimate competitors. You will need to compile a list of businesses that can (or do) have the greatest competitive effect on your company. Analyzing their strengths and weaknesses will give you insight into ways to outperform them and to find a specific customer need that is not well served. Your competitive analysis can also help you justify the marketing efforts you will need to capture your share of the market.

- Your research and analysis of the competition is critical to assessing your potential for success. You will have to find paying customers in two ways: 1) by drawing in those who don't regularly use your products and/or services, and 2) by taking customers away from the competition.

- Who are your customers? A powerful tool in developing your marketing concept is to create a customer profile based upon geographic, demographic, and economic data and personal observations.

- Do your customers need you? Your products and services should be developed and presented to customers as a solution to their needs. Tap in to the universal human condition by addressing such needs as hunger, pleasure, affordability, and convenience.

- Concentrate on solutions. The second half of the need-solution equation is how you will satisfy your customers' needs.

- Spend plenty of time setting your pricing. Setting appropriate prices requires a combination of financial analysis, competitive research, and demographic data. So how much should you charge? Will your customers be able to afford your products or services? Will they feel it is a fair price? Even wealthy customers look for a good value.

- Where your business "lives" can make or break it! Learn

as much about your potential customers and their buying habits to confirm that you have selected a prime location. A poor location may mean you will have to pay for more advertising.

- When establishing equipment budgets, compare what you want with what you need. How long will it take for the equipment to pay for itself? Will it positively affect your quality, service, or productivity? Could purchasing used equipment be smarter?

ORGANIZE YOUR RESEARCH

Creating a data-gathering and filing system from the get-go will save you time and make the writing process easier. Feel comfortable using it and make it a habit!

- Never leave home without:

  - **Notepad and pen** (or micro recorder) — All ideas have merit, so don't censor yourself. Leave your reminders here and follow up at the end of the day.

  - **Business cards** — Make it easy for people to get back to you with requested information.

  - **Expandable travel folder** — To collect information gathered throughout the day.

- Set up a business plan file cabinet.

- Create hanging files and file folders.

- Empty your pockets and travel folder daily. By taking

just a few minutes to review, sort, and file data gathered that day, you will be able to make notes and comments that may be lost to you weeks from now.

- Create a contact list.

  — Using either a small address book or an electronic personal digital assistant, start gathering and carrying your contact list.

  — Ask for a business card when you meet people.

  — Make notes to remind you why a contact can be helpful.

  — Note e-mail addresses and Web sites.

- Cross-index referrals. If Norman Taylor refers you to Betty Donaldson, make a note so you can "name drop" — "Hello, I'm doing research for a new business I am launching, and Norman Taylor of Taylor Accounting referred me to you as someone who might help me."

- Buy and send thank-you notes.

  — Your local stationery or office supply store will have professional-looking generic thank-you notes. Drop one in the mail when someone goes out of his or her way to provide assistance. This polite act is a great way to start a buzz within your community about your new business.

- Create a master to-do/reminder/follow-up list.

  — At the end of the day, transfer your notes and audio memos to a master list.

  — Research tends to turn up other research possibilities. Add these to your master to-do list.

- Create a "Business Plan Favorites" (bookmark) folder.

  — An enormous amount of research information is available on the Web. Create subtopic folders so you can categorize and find bookmarked sites quickly.

  — A great organizational tool for Web research is Onfolio at **www.onfolio.com**. Flag by importance, write reminder descriptions, search your notes by keyword, and even save text from a site and file it.

  — If you send e-mails requesting information, sort your outgoing messages and incoming responses into a "Business Plan" inbox folder. Check your e-mail client software for ways to make this automatic and to flag activity for you.

- Create a research list that consists of questions that you do not know the answers to right now. The answers should prove your business idea's viability.

- Remember, assumptions are not conclusions. When deciding what data you need to construct your business plan, don't make unnecessary assumptions. Assumptions, by definition, are personal beliefs not supported by fact. Assumptions are not a reliable foundation for decision-making and business success. If you believe something to be true, prove it. Unsupported claims may make your plan look strong, but they do everyone a disservice.

- Remember, conclusions are not assumptions. After researching your new plan, you must draw some conclusions. These conclusions aren't going to be 100 percent accurate; however, if they are fact-based and reasonable, they will convince potential lenders and investors that yours is a risk worth taking.

- Ask for help. Sometimes finding an answer can be difficult. However, one of the most powerful research tools is readily available to you at no cost: simply asking for help. Ask politely and give people ample time to respond. You will be surprised at what you can learn. The help you receive may also come in the form of opinions, recommendations, and referrals to other resources.

- You can hire help.

  - If the only free time you have to research your plan is after normal business hours, you will be depending primarily upon Web resources. Another option is to hire someone to assist with research. A professional researcher will have many resources from which to draw. To find a local researcher, use a search engine with the keyword "researcher" and your city name. Or contact your local library or college for a referral. University business departments may be able to connect you with a graduate student interested in handling your research needs. Professional market research firms such as Market Research (**www. marketresearch.com**) an d or BizVida (**www.bizvida. com**) can assist with a wide variety of research topics.

— Working with a certified public accountant (CPA) is worth every cent you will pay. Even the most seasoned businessperson could use some hands-on number crunching and advice when it comes to financial projects that span five years or more. Paying someone to create these necessary financial reports for your plan is fine; however, the most important aspect is to understand them and to be able to easily analyze each.

Make a wise investment in a couple of hours of one-on-one time with your CPA to learn accounting terms, how to read and interpret standard business reports (P&Ls, balance sheets, and various accounting formulas/ratios), and to develop intermediate financial decision-making skills.

Most small business startups are self-financed. Ninety-five percent of small business financing comes from personal resources.

4

INVESTING IN YOUR OWN DREAM

Whether you want to start a home-based business or build a 100-employee manufacturing plant, you will be your company's initial investor. In launching a new business, your personal financial history plays a critical role in obtaining credit, avoiding deposit fees, and outfitting your company. Although business experts advise against signing personal guarantees, it may be the only option until your business is credit-worthy.

All entrepreneurs dream of easy, low-interest loans; plentiful investors; and parents who ask, "How much do you need?" The truth is most small business startups are self-financed. Ninety-five percent of small business financing comes from personal resources, which means you need to look for every dime you can muster. The first place to start is with your credit.

YOUR PERSONAL FINANCIAL HEALTH

Often it is after losing one's job, returning from an extended absence from the workforce, or tiring of being underemployed that an employee begins to consider starting his or her own business. Each of these situations may have created some financial issues that need to be repaired, if possible. Improving your personal credit score will help you leverage your credit worthiness and underwrite your business venture.

The first step is to obtain a copy of your credit history and FICO score from the three largest credit reporting agencies — Experian, TransUnion, and Equifax. The federal Fair Credit Reporting Act (FCRA) requires these agencies to provide you with a free report every 12 months. For complete information, visit **www.ftc.gov/bcp/conline/pubs/credit/freereports.htm**.

FICO is a scoring system in which your debt-to-income ratio, total indebtedness, and other credit factors are reduced to a numerical credit score. The higher the score, the better your credit rating and the more likely you are to repay a loan. A strong FICO score means less potential risk for the lender and lower interest rates for you. To learn what your score means, visit FICO at **www.MyFICO.com**. Check the reports for accuracy. Credit issuers use the FICO score to assess your credit worthiness and income-to-debt ratio. To learn more about your credit rating and how improve it, see Chapter 19, "Resources."

Fix It

Upon reviewing your credit reports (be certain to obtain a detailed report, not just a FICO credit score), look for discrepancies and errors. Errors, which can range from a simple clerical error to a serious case of identity theft, are common, and it is up to the individual to dispute them. Each credit bureau has its own procedure for disputing reported financial activity, so you may have to file multiple disputes for the same creditor error.

If you received your credit report through the mail, information will be provided on how to request an investigation of a disputed listing. Investigations can also be filed online. Check the credit bureau's Web site (see Chapter 19) for complete instructions.

You will have to write a letter (or complete an online form) explaining why you believe a listing to be incorrect. If you have paperwork supporting your claim, send a copy along with your letter. Your letter should be sent via certified mail with a return receipt requested to prove mailing and receipt. Online claims typically are assigned an identifying number.

You may also want to contact the creditor, in writing, requesting a resolution to the error before filing a credit bureau investigation claim. If you do not receive a resolution within 30 days, start the credit bureau investigation procedure. Sometimes getting even obvious mistakes corrected can be difficult. Be diligent, and clearly document your case.

Clean It Up Yourself

There are legitimate nonprofit credit counseling services available. However, contact these only as a last resort. Their methods can get the bill collectors off your back and repay everyone, but using a credit counselor can negatively affect your credit score. If you determine you need credit counseling, contact the National Foundation for Credit Counseling (**www.nfcc.org**) for a legitimate referral. Do not pay anyone who promises to clean up your credit. The process is a do-it-yourself job.

Improve Your Credit Score

Even if your credit score is low because of valid credit problems, making some changes can boost your score. However, there is no fast way to improve your credit.

1. Contact your creditors about removing poor notations. If you have cleaned up your act, some creditors may be willing to remove older unfavorable entries for you. Keep your tone friendly and firm. If you are unsuccessful with the customer service person, ask to speak with a supervisor. Keep a log of your conversations. It takes time for changes to appear on your credit report, so it may benefit you to ask for a letter of confirmation.

2. Look for such errors as business obligations (which were not personally secured) mixed in with your personal data. Also watch for accounts that are not yours.

3. Do not close accounts in an effort to raise your credit score, as this typically has the opposite effect.

4. If you do cancel accounts, keep the oldest one open, as this gives you a longer history.

5. If you have credit cards close to being "maxed out," transfer balances to reduce the percentage of used versus available credit. The amount of "available" credit on a card is a plus for you.

6. Try "rapid rescoring." In this process, legitimate corrections and credit card payoffs are updated quickly with the credit bureau for a fee. You cannot do this by yourself; you'll need to find a lender who is a customer of a rapid rescoring service to handle this on your behalf.

The fee can run as much as $75 for every account that needs to be adjusted; however, this could make the difference in obtaining a lower interest rate.

CREATE AN ASSET LIST

Anything of value that can be converted to cash is an asset. If you earnestly want to raise money to start a business, look at every potential source for cash. Converting assets to cash means selling them for the best price you can get. Thanks to the Web and such sites as eBay, Yahoo auctions, and Half.com, selling personal possessions has never been easier.

Start compiling your personal asset list, but remember that cashing in insurance policies, bonds, and other investments is risky.

ASSET LIST

Asset Category	Items with Potential Value	Converting to Cash
Cash	Savings and checking	Not required.
College funds	College savings	Beware; raiding college funds can be too "easy" and are difficult to replace.
Investments	Stocks, bonds, mutual funds, etc.	
Retirement	401k, pension plans, Roth IRA, IRA	Beware; may trigger federal and state tax penalties and income taxes.
Insurance	Life insurance	
Home(s)	Home, rental property, vacation homes	

Asset Category	Items with Potential Value	Converting to Cash
Vehicles	Recreation vehicles/property	
Antiques and collectibles	Artwork, coins, stamps, sports memorabilia, books	EBay, consignment shops.
Personal possessions	Household goods, clothing, electronics, etc.	Garage sale, consignment shops, classified ads, eBay.

OTHER ASSETS

Other Ways to Raise (or Save) Cash

- Collect on outstanding debts owed to you.

- Ask for deposit refunds from utilities.

- Take advantage of all early-pay or cash discounts.

- Whenever possible, avoid delivery or shipping charges.

- Join a co-op or buying group.

- Open wholesale accounts and ask for commercial discounts.

- Negotiate long-term customer discounts based upon future purchases.

For some home businesses, a successful garage sale may be enough to pay for the necessary business licenses, equipment, and business cards to get you started.

BARTERING

Bartering is an age-old way to obtain products and services with no or minimal cash. Although bartering is still a taxable activity based on value exchanges, it can be an excellent way to obtain what you need now, allowing you to deal with the tax implications later. Your accountant can advise you on how bartered transactions are taxed.

Bartering can be done on an informal basis directly between you and local suppliers or through a barter exchange. Barter exchanges have an advantage in that you can earn "points" that can be spent with other exchange members. For more information, see Chapter 19, "Resources."

Let's say you sell computer printers and you need some photography for a brochure. Through the exchange you find someone who needs a printer. The exchange is made and you receive 1,000 barter points that you spend with a local commercial photographer. The commercial photographer uses the 1,000 barter points you "paid" him to obtain the business cards he needs and has points left for another need.

When bartering, be specific about what you have to offer and what you seek. Agree on the value of each item traded. When exploring bartering, be aware that "over-bartering" can adversely affect your cash flow.

Universally, more than half of all startup capital comes from family and friends. In fact, experts believe family or friend loans and investments easily exceed all monies invested by venture capitalists.

Neither a Borrower nor a Lender Be

These wise words from William Shakespeare offer sound fiscal advice, but the bard was actually referring to the personal problems borrowing can create: "For loan oft loses both itself and friend."

To make your entrepreneurial dreams come true, you may have to visit the Bank of Mom and Dad. Universally, more than half of all startup capital comes from family and friends. In fact, experts believe family or friend loans and investments easily exceed all monies invested by venture capitalists.

Because this is such an important source of financing, consider all the implications. Family or friend financing can be through a loan, a gift, or an investment. This chapter will explore each and help you avoid potential pitfalls.

SHOULD YOU ASK?

To follow are some things you should think about before you ask your family or a friend to help finance your business venture.

1. Is there money available? Not all families are open and honest about their financial status, so money may not be available for lending.

2. Do you feel "entitled?" Money can cloud your judgment, trigger "entitlement" issues, and create animosity, particularly among siblings.

3. Can they afford to "lose" the money? Should your business fail, will they be at financial risk?

4. Will you treat them as a creditor? When cash gets tight, will you let payments slide because they'll "understand" better than the bank?

5. Could you lose a friend or alienate a relative? If you are unable to repay the debt or if the investment doesn't yield what you promised, will it affect your relationship?

6. Is it a loan, a gift, or an inheritance "payout?" Be clear and formalize the transaction. A written "statement of gift" or contract will clarify the transaction. If it is a loan, you want to be able to deduct the interest. If it is a gift, you will need to meet IRS regulations to avoid additional taxes.

7. Can you protect their investment? Unless your relative is a professional investor or banker, he or she probably isn't appropriately cautious about assessing the risk. Likewise, accepting money from people you care about increases your responsibility to accept and spend it wisely.

KNOW HOW MUCH YOU NEED

When seeking financial support, determine how much you need, when you need it, and when you can repay it. Inadequate financing and poor cash flow increases your family's or friend's financial risk. As you review your plan and assess your potential for success, factor in the personal costs of losing their investment or gift.

BORROWING FROM FAMILY OR FRIENDS

Borrowing from relatives or friends can be the easiest (and sometimes the only) way to accumulate enough seed money for your new business venture. Whether you need $1,000 or $100,000, it is in everyone's best interest to follow sound business practices when borrowing from acquaintances. It is tempting to be lax and forget to sign a contract or not set an appropriate repayment schedule. Borrowing money on a handshake can create problems for you later on. Here are some reasons why you should negotiate fair loan terms and sign a formal loan document:

- You want to deduct the interest as a business expense. A contract or promissory note is your proof to the IRS that this is a legitimate business loan and not a personal loan where interest is not tax-deductible.

- You want the IRS to consider this as a loan. The IRS has regulations regarding gifts and loans. For this financial change to be considered a loan you will need to:

  — Have an enforceable agreement such as a promissory note.

— Pay an appropriate interest rate. Low- or no-interest loans may be classified as gifts, thus triggering gift taxation rules.

— Have a reasonable repayment schedule. Loans with no repayment schedules also may be deemed as gifts.

— The lender must include interest paid as other income.

LOAN AGREEMENTS

Technically, your loan agreement can be a verbal commitment; however, getting it in writing is a much smarter way to do business. If you are uncertain what necessary elements should be outlined in the note, seek legal advice.

Promissory Notes

A promissory note is a written promise to repay a set amount within a set period plus a specific amount of interest. It does not need to be notarized to be valid and can be completed by both parties. For smaller dollar amounts with simple terms, a do-it-yourself promissory note may be all you need. You and the lender will sign one original, which is usually kept by the lender. Once you repay the note, the original is returned to the borrower.

You can find fill-in-the-blank promissory notes at your local stationery or office supply store, as part of business form software packages, or free online at Internet Legal Research Group (**www.ilrg.com/forms/promisry.html**).

For larger sums and more complicated repayment terms and conditions, you should have an attorney prepare the note. It is also in your best interest to have an attorney review any loan agreement prepared by the other party.

Lending Circle (**www.circlelending.com**) is an online resource for financial transactions between family and friends. For a fee, this service will prepare and administer (accept payments) your promissory notes for a fee.

ASKING FOR A LOAN

Here are ten guidelines to help you obtain financial support from family and friends. Remember that this is a business transaction based on your personal pledge of repayment; failing to honor your commitments can end friendships and divide families.

1. Start by explaining your idea, using your "elevator pitch," and ask if they might be interested in providing some financial support.

2. Make an appointment for an appropriate time to talk and share your business plan.

3. Provide a copy of your complete business plan to be read later.

4. Be prepared to discuss your commitment and intentions. Assure them that you are entering this arrangement with a signed note and consider this a business deal.

5. Do not let your excitement improperly color your presentation. It is easy to get overly excited and overstate the potential for success when you are talking to friends or family members. You want them to enter into this arrangement knowing all the facts.

6. Make a full disclosure. When presenting yourself and your business plan to a professional lender or investor, you will do everything you can to present your case positively and honestly. It is wise when dealing with a friend or family member to be as open and honest as possible. You want the money, but you don't want them to make a poor financial decision.

7. Understand that borrowing from family and friends almost always comes with hidden strings. Your personal connection opens the door to unsolicited advice, unspoken expectations, and disappointments. However, it can also be a wise investment with ample rewards for everyone.

8. Schedule a time to return to discuss your plan along with repayment terms and potential investment earnings. Return with a promissory note outlining all details. Encourage them to have their attorney review the document before signing.

9. Don't make assumptions that a friend or relative will overlook a late payment or that the loan will "disappear" should your business fail.

10. If this is an early payout of a trust or inheritance, see your attorney and your accountant regarding tax and inheritance implications.

THANKS FOR THE GIFT

Depending upon your family circumstances, your proposal to borrow money for your business may be answered with, "How about if we give you the money?" Often parents and other relatives continue to feel a sense of responsibility for the well-being of their adult children; others simply enjoy sharing the wealth and helping you realize your dreams. Few gifts, however, are without strings.

The first strings may be the hidden or implied ones that parents can attach. Will the money be spent wisely? Do you really need that much? Why don't we give you the money and you can hire your younger sister too? You know your family dynamics — what strings might make this gift unacceptable for you?

Keep in mind that there are federal tax laws regarding financial gifts, and some states have gift taxes. Gift taxes occur when you transfer any property (including money) to another without expecting something of at least equal value in return. If your mother deeds you a piece of property to build your business, this is considered a gift.

The IRS works from the viewpoint that all gifts are taxable with exceptions, such as:

- The gift is less than the annual exclusion amount (in 2005, this is $11,000 per giver, so your mother and father together could give you $22,000 before it becomes taxable).

- The gift is from a spouse.

- The gift is to a qualified political or charitable organization.

- The gift pays for tuition or medical expenses.

For gifts worth more than the annual exclusion, refer to IRS Publication 950, Introduction to Estate and Gift Taxes. Your investment counselor, attorney, or CPA should be consulted regarding taxable gifts.

These gifts are not tax-deductible for the giver.

MONEY FROM TRUSTS AND INHERITANCES

There are many different types of living trusts through which family assets are administered, each with its own set of stipulations. Before withdrawing funds from these, speak with your financial adviser as to potential penalties and tax obligations.

Usually an inheritance is willed after the death of a loved one. However, like living trusts, inheritance trusts are set up to administer assets that will be passed on at death. These assets are not passed on to individuals but to the trust. If the funds are coming from a family member's inheritance trust, the administering trustee will outline the proper procedure or changes required for an early distribution.

6

YOUR LOAN PROPOSAL

Loans are about trust and risk. Lenders want to trust that the loan will be repaid and to risk as little as possible. Your loan request should be a reasonable amount, documenting how the money will be spent and that you will meet the scheduled payments.

The loan proposal acts as your ambassador. Even if a lender believes in you, agrees your business is worth the risk, and is impressed by your business savvy, other decision-makers in the organization may not agree. Ultimately, it comes down to your loan proposal.

MORE THAN AN APPLICATION

You have probably obtained a mortgage, car loan, or credit card, so you are familiar with loan applications. Commercial lenders will have a standard loan application form that you will complete, and SBA-backed loans usually have a complete application package. A few lines on a form cannot tell the story of why you should be granted the loan, so many lenders allow you to provide additional documentation that supports your ability to repay the debt, explains potential problems, and builds confidence in your business concept.

A good proposal will contain everything the lender needs to know in order to be convinced that you are a competent entrepreneur, that your business is capable of growth, and that you are not a high credit risk. Be complete, neat, and organized.

Many loan proposals are immediately rejected simply because they are messy. Most lenders refuse to sift through disorganized paperwork. It reflects poorly on your business and indicates a potential management problem.

Essential Components of a Loan Proposal

Including a full business plan with your proposal is a good way for lenders to get to know your business. Of course, the plan should be modified to suit the needs of the lenders, as opposed to the needs of investors.

Loan Request Summary

1. No longer than two to four pages.

2. The amount you hope to borrow.

3. How the money will be used.

4. Type of loan applied for (line of credit, term loan, etc.).

5. Repayment schedule and source of repayment.

6. Collateral offered.

7. Financial performance summaries; past, present, and projected.

FINANCIAL STATEMENTS

The type of financial statements you must provide depends on the stage of growth of your business.

Startup Businesses

1. Projected balance sheets and income statements for the next three years.

2. Owners' personal financial statements.

3. Social Security numbers for checking owners' credit reports.

4. Detailed information about the collateral pledged.

Established Small Businesses

1 Historical balance sheets and income statements from the past three years.

2. Projections for the next three years.

3. CPA-audited financial statement or tax returns, depending on the lender's needs.

4. Owners' personal financial statements.

Larger Businesses

1. Historical balance sheets and income statements from the past three to five years.

2. Projections for the next three to five years.

3. CPA-audited financial statement, assuring that your financial statements conform to GAAP (generally accepted accounting principles) standards.

4. Owners' personal financial statements.

Make sure your projected balance sheets, income statements, and cash flow projections are achievable. The lender will often condition the loan based on calculations from your projections, so don't think you won't be held to them. Break down the projections for the first year by month. Projections for following years may be broken down quarterly.

Summarize key points for the lender on a separate summary page. Also include a page of explanations for anything in your financial statements that might be misinterpreted. This will prevent the lender from making any false assumptions about the status of your business. Clarify — up front — anything you think might be misinterpreted.

You may also include the following:

1. Collateral value summary.

2. Appraisals of property.

3. Inventory value summary.

4. Accounts receivable and payable summaries will help the lender determine both how long it takes customers to pay you and how long it takes you to pay suppliers.

Researching your lender's specific financing guidelines and providing the necessary information in an organized and efficient manner expedites the loan process.

YOUR FINANCIAL STATEMENTS

Keeping track of a business's accounts can be a complicated endeavor, which is why most businesses keep an accountant on staff or use an accounting firm.

When doing business, every transaction needs to be documented, tracked, and organized, making it much easier to compile financial statements at the end of the month, quarter, or year.

The four most common types of financial statements and their components are:

The Income Statement

COMPONENTS

1. Categorized revenues from a single business period.

2. Categorized expenses from a single business period.

3. Difference from revenues and expenses indicating net income or net loss.

APPLICATIONS

1. Represents bottom line.

2. Indicates where money is being spent.

3. Indicates where money is coming from.

Statement of Capital

COMPONENTS

1. Owner's capital account (how much of the business he or she owns).

2. Net income or net loss from a single business period (as derived from income statement).

3. Change in owner's capital account based on net income or net loss (any net income becomes the owner's).

APPLICATIONS

1. Helps owner to decide whether to reinvest net income, keep some profit as personal income, or withdraw completely.

2. Indicates to owner whether or not his or her personal stake is at risk.

The Balance Sheet

COMPONENTS

1. Listing of all current assets (everything a business owns).

2. Listing of all current liabilities (everything a business owes to creditors).

3. Value of owner's capital account.

4. Company's financial condition (liabilities + owner's equity = assets).

APPLICATIONS

1. Indicates a company's financial condition at a specific moment in time, as opposed to a full business period.

2. Helps owner get a clear picture of assets and liabilities.

Cash Flow Statement

COMPONENTS

1. Categorized list of all sources of income for business (sales of assets, revenues, financing, etc.).

2. Categorized list of ways income is used (purchases, debt repayment, operating losses, etc.).

APPLICATIONS

1. Indicates whether business's cash flow is increasing or decreasing.

2. Helps owner monitor possible cash flow problems.

Financial statements are like a heart monitor for business. Without them, it would be impossible to recognize downward trends or to know when to enact countermeasures to reverse these trends.

Work with an accountant to make sure you understand these documents. Otherwise, you may not notice the early warning signs of an impending disaster.

Having accurate financial documents also can help you gain financing, as these statements are often included in your business plan or loan proposal. Investors and bankers are going to feel more comfortable about investing in a business that keeps track of its money in an organized and communicable way.

FINANCIAL STATEMENTS

After you have completed your business plan, you will know your current and future financial needs. Once you have determined how much money is needed at each stage, look for sources of financing.

No matter how much capital you need to launch a new business, your personal financial resources are the first place to look. Investors and lenders won't come on board unless you have made a significant financial commitment.

HOW TO WRITE A LOAN PROPOSAL

Approval of your loan request depends on how well you present yourself, your business, and your financial needs to a lender. Remember, lenders want to make loans, but they must make loans they know will be repaid. The best way to improve your chances of obtaining a loan is to prepare a written proposal.

A well-written loan proposal contains:

General Information

1. Business name, names of principals, Social Security number for each principal, and the business address.

2. Purpose of the loan — Exactly what the loan will be used for and why it is needed.

3. Amount required — The exact amount you need to achieve your purpose.

Business Description

1. History and nature of the business, including details of what kind of business it is, its age, number of employees, and current business assets.

2. Ownership structure, detailing the company's legal form.

Management Profile

1. Develop a short statement on each principal in your business; provide background, education, experience, skills, and accomplishments.

Market Information

1. Clearly define your company's products as well as your markets.

2. Identify your competition and explain how your business competes in the marketplace.

3. Profile your customers and explain how your business can satisfy their needs.

Financial Information

1. Financial statements — Balance sheets and income statements for the past three years. If you are starting out, provide a projected balance sheet and income statement.

2. Personal financial statements on yourself and other principal owners of the business.

3. Collateral you would be willing to pledge as security for the loan.

HOW YOUR LOAN REQUEST WILL BE REVIEWED

When reviewing a loan request, the lender is primarily concerned about repayment. To help determine this ability, many loan officers will order a copy of your business credit report from a credit reporting agency. Therefore, work with these agencies to help them present an accurate picture of your business.

Using the credit report and the information you have provided, the lending officer will consider the following issues:

1. Have you invested savings or personal equity in your business totaling at least 25 to 50 percent of the loan you are requesting? A lender or investor will not finance 100 percent of your business.

2. Do you have a sound record of creditworthiness as indicated by your credit report, work history, and letters of recommendation?

3. Do you have sufficient experience and training to operate a successful business?

4. Have you prepared a loan proposal and business plan that demonstrate your understanding of and commitment to the success of the business?

5. Does the business have sufficient cash flow to make the monthly payments?

CHAPTER 7

VALUATION OF YOUR BUSINESS

AN ELUSIVE FIGURE

It is commonly understood that "value" is subjective. An old rocking chair might look like soon-to-be kindling to one person but an irreplaceable treasure to another. Perception and emotional connections also make it difficult to establish a value for your business. However, value really all comes down to money—how much can be made and what are the risks.

Valuation is necessary to attract investors. Investors are far more likely to put money into companies with higher valuations. It doesn't matter what *you* think your company is worth; it matters what *investors* think your company is worth.

There are as many ways to value a company as there are companies. Part of valuation is determining the most similar or consistent aspect of an industry, and using that aspect of the individual company to define a significant part of its value. Businesses are also valued on what they might be worth in the future. After all, the investor's primary concern is getting a return on their investment, which means the business must be valuable in the future.

It is important to note that valuation is not a hard science; rather, it is more like an elaborate educated guess. The valuation method you use can have a tremendous impact on how your business looks to investors.

Please note that while you want to make the business look good, you also want to give the most accurate representation of the business as possible. If you can't deliver what you promise to investors, you will pay for it in the long run. Not to mention, you will have ruined your chance of getting the next round of funding from the same investors. Exaggerating the worth of your business just to gain capital can definitely get you into a lot of trouble.

Investors will also attempt to value your company lower, or discount the valuation more than it should be, to save money. They will be able to buy more of your equity for less if the valuation happens to be on the lower side of the spectrum.

There may also be certain market factors that will affect the valuation of your business. Trends in technology are usually the major factor. For instance, when Xerox purchased Scientific Data Systems in the late 1960s, SDS had $100 million in sales and earned about $10 million after taxes. However, Xerox bought the company for $10 billion. Obviously, their valuation of the company was influenced by the belief that this small firm's growth was going to explode.

This trend of large corporations buying out small firms with little or no revenues continues to this day, making many a small business owner very rich indeed. It is in these examples that we see just how subjective valuation can be.

COMPARABLES

As with real estate, appraising a business often involves comparables (also known as comps) to help determine the fair market value of a business by comparing it to one or more other similar businesses. Fair market value is usually assumed to be how much the business would sell for if both the buyer and seller were willing and equally informed about the state of the business.

Comparables are the simplest way to get a general sense of what a company is worth. Also known as the market approach, it is not the only way a business must be valued by an investor or venture capital firm. Many variables must be quantified and compared in order to get a more accurate picture. Also, if the market moves very quickly, the valuation of your comparable may be obsolete by the time it gets to your desk.

The easiest way to think of comparables is to think of your business as a product. You have a product you wish to sell, it so you need to know how much to charge for it. To see what the market will bear, study similar products. Immediately, the problems with using comparables become evident. For example, your factory is farther from your largest customers, so there are additional transportation costs getting your product to market, or you have less (or more) packaging requirements to get your product safely in your customers' hands.

Because different features and benefits must be considered, you have to adjust the baseline figure your comps provided to achieve more accurate representation of what the product is truly worth.

The comparable must match up with your company in several important ways:

- The business must be close enough in size to your own.

- The business must operate in a similar fashion.

- The business must be in the same industry, serving the same market.

- The business must use similar accounting methods.

- The business must project similar growth.

For publicly owned comparable businesses, their value is based on stock prices. To figure the value of the company it is being compared to, the stock price is usually divided by two types of earnings, like net income and sales, then the book value. What this market approach does not take into account, however, is that some companies are just better than others. It makes sense that if you do a better job than a company in the same industry that is the same size as you, your fair market value should be higher than theirs.

Usually, if you are looking for capital, it means you have faith that you can make your business grow. The comparable is a simple way to see what your business's chances might be given the current market conditions of your industry. Comparables, when valid, can be very useful, but it is important to remember where they fall short.

Sometimes comparables are simply not practical. For instance:

- You cannot find a business that is similar to yours.

- The business to which yours is compared is poorly run.

- Your industry is going through extreme ups or downs and the valuation is obsolete after a week.

Many investors will not be satisfied with a simple comparable, no matter how relevant or valid it may seem. Investors must rely on a number of different perspectives and look at the valuation from as many angles as possible before deciding a company's worth.

Investors will employ one of many other, more complex valuation methods to try to forecast what the business will be worth in the future, and whether the risk is too great or the return too small.

These methods include, but are not limited to the following:

- The venture capital method.

- The First Chicago method.

- Ownership dilution.

- Discounted cash flow (or "the income approach").

- Asset appraisal.

The Venture Capital Method

The venture capital method relies on the company being sold or going public at some future time and forecasting what the company will be worth at the time of this future sale. In other words, the method works backward from what it is assumed the company will be worth in five or ten years or whenever it is sold or goes public.

Obviously, no one knows what the company is actually going

to be worth in five or ten years, but by looking at companies in the same industry today that are undergoing an initial public offering (IPO) and figuring out how much they were worth five or ten years ago, you can get a multiple based in fact and then apply it to your own company's figures.

Investors will not assume that your business will do as well as the businesses on which the multiple was based. After factoring risks, past performance, and how eager you are for capital, they will discount the multiple substantially to bring down the value of your business. This makes equity in your company less expensive for the investor. It is important for you be confident that the discount was calculated fairly.

The First Chicago Method

A variation on the venture capital method, the First Chicago method is named after the bank holding company that first employed it. Instead of using one scenario to create a multiple and then discounting it based on risk, this method uses a best-, most likely, and worst-case scenario and then averages the three to create its multiple.

This can help an investor reach a decision about whether or not to invest in a company by accounting for possible failure. Of course, as with all valuation methods that are engaged in prediction, it shouldn't be taken as an exact or scientific assessment.

Ownership Dilution

This factor is usually taken into account as a supplement to the venture capital method. The investor understands that this is not the only round of funding the company is likely to need. In order to maintain their equity percentage, they must participate in those subsequent rounds.

This process predicts how much the investor's percentage would be diluted if they did not participate. Although some investors may be prepared to help with future financing, others might want to take their return and run. This will affect how much dilution discounts the value.

Discounted Cash Flow

This method, also known as the income approach, values a company based on how well it generates income. Since money changes value over time, the discount is applied to cover the risk involved.

The investor states the rate of return and provides money based on your projected cash flow less the return rate, but anticipating to be repaid the full amount. The trade off is that you get the money now, but you end up paying more for it.

Asset Appraisal

A more basic approach, the asset appraisal is simply a calculation of the value of every tangible item the business owns. By adding the value of all business property, including vehicles, office equipment, and so on, the investor can get a clear picture of the scope of your operation.

Choosing debt or equity, or a combination of both, to finance your business depends on many factors. The first step is understanding the pros and cons of acquiring debt and sharing equity.

CHAPTER

8

DEBT FINANCING VERSUS EQUITY FINANCING

C hoosing debt or equity, or a combination of both, to finance your business depends on many factors. The first step is understanding the pros and cons of acquiring debt and sharing equity. Debt financing means you take on a loan, note, or other repayable debt in exchange for receiving funds. The repayment terms are fixed. Equity financing means you receive financing funds in exchange for capital stock, stock options, or other ownership activities. Because the lender shares ownership of your company, they also share profits without any guaranteed return.

Loans and lines of credit are straightforward business transactions in which you know exactly what you receive and when you must repay it. However, if you think your business's cash flow may not be able to keep up with the payments required by debt, you might want to approach investors who will not expect returns for several years. Conversely, if you want to maintain total control of your business and retain any future profits and you project steady cash flow, debt is the better option. Once you pay the loan, the profits are yours to keep.

FINANCING TYPES

Types of Debt Financing

- Long-term bank loans

- Short-term bank loans

- SBA loans

- Lines of credit

- Leasing versus buying

- Inventory financing

- Customer financing

- Factoring receivables

- Home-equity loans

- Corporate bonds

- Letters of credit

- Credit cards

Types of Equity Financing

- Family and friends

- Angel investors

- Strategic investors

- Strategic partnering

- Founder capital

- Venture capital

- Small business investment companies (SBICs)

- Employee stock ownership plans (ESOPs)

DEBT FINANCING

Although the idea of funding a venture exclusively with other people's money sounds attractive, it rarely happens. It is extremely unusual for a business owner to have zero financial risk. Investors prefer to see that the founder has a personal stake in the business, whether it is a home used as collateral or a substantial amount of personal savings invested. For the most part, most lenders and investors prefer a debt-equity ratio of one, which means that for every dollar of debt, there is a dollar of the owner's money invested as equity.

Debt financing is the natural choice for most startup and early-stage businesses. No control over the business is lost, and successfully making your monthly payments on time can help you procure future debt financing. The important thing, then, is to make sure the loan is arranged favorably for your business.

Here are some things to consider before applying for or accepting a loan:

- Your credit status. What chance does your business have of qualifying for debt financing?

- The size of the loan. Will it be big enough to suit your needs and help you grow?

- Your cash flow projections. Are they accurate enough to be relied upon to pay down the debt each month?

- Interest rates and market conditions. Can you still satisfy the loan conditions if the market slows down or if interest rates go up?

- Sources of collateral. Will you stake personal or company assets as collateral?

- Business plan and financial documents. Is all the paperwork in order, and does it accurately reflect the status of the business? Does the business plan need to be revised?

- Terms and conditions. Are they favorable? If not, are there other financing options to explore?

The good news is that everything you earn after paying off the debt is yours to keep. The bad news is that if you can't keep up with monthly payments, you will be in serious trouble with your bank. Your credit rating will suffer as well. You may even be forced to liquidate your assets to pay off the debt.

The biggest obstacles for debt financing are qualifying for a loan and having adequate collateral before you can get the capital you need. It helps to have some of your own money in the business, as this shows the bank that you have put personal assets on the line.

Exercise caution when using debt financing, as having too much debt decreases your financial leverage. This means that your debt-equity ratio becomes too high, requiring your business to make a large sum of money each period solely to service the debt.

As much as debt seems like a burden, it is still the most likely source of startup capital. Debt is less expensive in the long run, and makes finding investors less expensive too, once you have proven that your business is not high risk. Unless you are extremely lucky or have a knockout loan proposal, you are likely to meet with a fair share of rejection from banks. If the rejection is a result of poor cash flow projections, then another financing option may be the best alternative.

EQUITY FINANCING

When considering equity financing, keep in mind the long-term effects it will have on your business. Investors tend to remain only until they get a return on their investment. Keep in mind that selling off equity cannot be reversed easily.

In addition, if you sell too much equity too early in your company's existence, you will not have ample equity to work with during future rounds of financing. More important, when your company succeeds, you will have already sold your future profits!

Attracting investors can be extremely difficult, particularly for a startup with great risk potential. If your business is already established or if you do not qualify for debt financing, equity financing might be your best bet. Equity financing can help businesses grow faster, because an investor does not expect a return for several years, freeing up capital that would have gone into monthly payments had debt financing been used.

In exchange for providing the business with capital, the investor assumes partial ownership of the business. Depending on how the deal is arranged, the investor may also assume some of the control and provide additional management support. However, equity deals are also established in which the investor owns most of the business, but has none of the control. The investor's returns, when they come, are usually higher than the amount of interest you would pay a lender because the investor has assumed greater risk.

Be prepared to regularly update the investor on how the business is doing, how their money is spent, and whether or not they are on schedule to receive their return.

A few things to consider before undertaking equity financing:

- Will you be able to attract investors?

- Will investors pay enough for partial ownership to meet your financial needs?

- As an owner, are you willing to share control?

- Are you comfortable with sharing trade secrets and ideas with potential investors?

- Is your business plan current, accurate, and geared toward the potential investor?

- Does your business stay on top of its records, making it easy to keep the investor informed?

- How much of the future profit are you willing to share?

So which option is right for your business? It depends on what you qualify for and on what your expectations are. For instance:

- Do you want to grow quickly? Are you comfortable sharing ownership? Could you use a fresh face at your next board meeting? If yes, equity should be your choice.

- Do you want to stay in control of your business and keep all of your profits? Is your business well-leveraged? Are you uncomfortable with an investor expecting frequent updates on the status of the business? If yes, then debt financing is for you.

In assessing the options, make sure you understand the necessary compromises as well as where you absolutely cannot compromise. In seeking the dollars you need, you may find that a combination of loans and investment money provides the balance between debt and equity that you can best afford.

Here are a few guidelines to help determine whether you should pursue a loan agreement or sell equity to raise capital.

- If you have a high ratio of equity to debt, you probably can afford debt financing.

- If you have a greater debt-to-equity ratio, you probably should seek equity financing.

- Debt financing may require your personal guarantee. Consider how this will affect your personal credit.

- Review your cash flow analysis. Will you be able to meet payments every month? Equity financing preserves cash.

- Is your need greater than your fiscal power? Often new businesses are incapable of borrowing sufficient capital to support their launch before seeing their first profits. In that case, you will need equity financing.

- Do you have enough time to secure equity financing?

The Small Business Administration helps small businesses obtain financing to launch or grow their businesses. The SBA plays a crucial role in helping thousands of small businesses secure the funding they need.

CHAPTER 9

UNCLE SAM
HELPS OUT

I n 1953, Congress chartered the Small Business
Administration (SBA) to help small businesses obtain
the financing needed to launch or grow their businesses.
The SBA plays a crucial role in helping thousands of small
businesses secure the funding they need through underwriting
loan subsidies along with business development resources and
entrepreneurship training.

In 2004, the SBA backed more than $12.3 billion in small
business loans. Additionally, more than $1 billion was spent
on small business disaster loans. The SBA also assisted small
businesses in securing over some $40 billion in federal contracts.

The SBA is not a direct lender; SBA loans actually come from
SBA-approved commercial lenders. The SBA acts as a co-signer,
pledging to repay up to 85 percent of the loan should you
default. This reduces the lender's risk, making it easier to grant
funding for riskier business ventures.

The primary small business loan guaranty programs currently
being funded by Congress are the 7(a) Loan Guaranty Program,
the Certified Development Company (CDC), a 504 program,

and Microloan, and a 7(m) program. Each SBA program is governed by different regulations. Which program a business should use depends on:

- Standards of eligibility

- Amount of loan required

- Repayment terms and conditions

- Loan capital usage restrictions

- Approval process of borrower

THE 7(A) LOAN GUARANTY PROGRAM

As the main loan guaranty program of the SBA, the 7(a) can be used by businesses for startup financing, to restructure debt, to acquire or improve assets, or as a form of working capital. The repayment period depends on how the loan proceeds are used.

- Purchasing real estate. Loans used for real estate can be repaid over a maximum period of 25 years.

- Equipment purchases. Loans used to buy new equipment can be repaid over a period of 15 years, or for the life span of the equipment purchased, whichever is shorter.

- Working capital. If the business is using the loan as working capital, they have a maximum period of seven years to repay it.

The Guarantee

The SBA guarantees up to 85 percent of the loan amount for loans under $150,000 and 75 percent of the loan for loans over

$150,000 (up to a loan maximum of $1.5 million). The lender finances your business, based upon its company guidelines, once the government guarantee is in place.

SBAExpress loans have a maximum 50 percent guarantee. Export Working Capital loans carry a 90 percent loan guarantee up to $1 million.

The Interest

SBA funding is neither free money (grants) nor are the interest rates subsidized. You can expect to pay current business rates (fixed or variable) as set by the lender; however, there are maximum interest rate rules based upon the prime rate.

As of May 2005:

- Interest on fixed rate loans of $50,000 or more cannot exceed prime plus 2.25 percent if the loan matures in less than seven years or prime plus 2.75 percent if the loan matures after seven years.

- Interest on loans between $25,000 and $50,000 cannot exceed prime plus 3.25 percent if loan matures in less than seven years or prime plus 3.75 percent if the maturity is seven years or more.

- Interest on loans of $25,000 or less cannot exceed prime plus 4.25 percent if the loan matures in less than seven years or prime plus 4.75 percent if the maturity is seven years or more.

For current 7(a) program terms, visit the SBA Web site at **www.sba.gov/financing/sbaloan/7a.html**.

Maturity Schedules

The length of an SBA-backed loan is based upon an established formula determining the life of the assets purchased and the borrower's ability to repay. Loan funds used for multiple purposes have a weighted average maturity date with equal monthly payments.

Purpose of Loan	Loan Life
Machinery and equipment	10 to 25 years
Buildings (purchase or construction)	Up to 25 years
Working capital	7 to 10 years

7(a) Eligibility

The first step in applying for an SBA loan is finding out if you are eligible. You must be considered a small business according to the specific size standard the SBA has set for your particular industry. In some industries this is determined by annual revenues; in others, by the number of employees.

To find out if you are eligible, you need to know your SIC (Standard Industrial Code) classification, which may be obtained by visiting the U.S. Department of Labor Occupational Safety & Health Administration at **www.osha.gov/pls/imis/ sicsearch.html**. This code is how the SBA determines the maximum number of employees or total revenue a business in a certain industry can have in order to qualify for a 7(a) loan.

Below are the general size guidelines for eligibility:

- Wholesale companies with fewer than 100 employees.

- Agricultural companies with sales of less than $750,000.

- Retail or service companies with not more than $29 million annual sales (three-year average). Sales limits are based on your business type.

- Manufacturers with fewer than 500 employees (as many as 1,500 in some cases).

- Construction companies with no more than $28.5 million annual sales (three-year average). Sales limits are based on your business type.

Once determined to be a small business, you must demonstrate that you have exhausted alternative forms of funding, including personal assets. Your business must operate in the United States and be a for-profit entity. Finally, the owner's equity must be enough so that investment can occur in the future.

The Application Package

The paperwork required for a regular 7(a) loan is quite complicated. The SBA estimates that it will take about 25 hours to complete the entire application package. Once you review the application, you may decide that you need some help in completing everything. Low- or no-cost assistance may be available through local small business development (city, county, or state) agencies. Other nonprofit agencies such as SCORE also provide loan advice.

Professional loan preparers can complete your SBA loan package. As with hiring any consultant, carefully screen for both experience and professionalism. Beware of anyone who guarantees SBA approval. Your lender may be able to provide you with a referral after receiving the bank's commitment. You should expect to pay between $1,200 to $5,000 for their services.

Prequalification Program

To help business owners create their loan application packages and secure a loan, the SBA created a Prequalification Program. The program is aimed at low-income borrowers, disabled business owners, new businesses, emerging markets, veterans, exporters, rural, and specialized industries. Under the program, an SBA intermediary is assigned to work with you to review your business plan as well as to determine your eligibility and credit worthiness. If the intermediary believes your application has a good chance for approval, he or she will send it to the SBA for expedited processing.

The SBA review and analysis will follow the standard time frame; however, upon approval, the SBA will issue a commitment (prequalification) letter stating that the SBA is willing to guarantee the loan made by a commercial lender. Your intermediary can then help you locate a lender that meets your needs and offers the most competitive rates.

The maximum loan amount for this pilot program is $250,000, and all other policies, procedures, and requirements follow the standard 7(a) loan program.

Your Personal Guarantee

One condition of 7(a) loans is that all owners, who own 20 percent or more of the company, personally guarantee SBA loans.

Prohibited Fees

The SBA prohibits your bank from charging you loan fees that are typical of business and personal loans. These fees include processing fees, application fees, loan origination fees, points, brokerage fees, and bonus fees. The only commitment fee allowed is applicable under the Export Working Capital Loan Program.

Prepayment Fees

Paying your SBA loan off before its maturity date may be subject your business to a "subsidy recoupment" or prepayment fee. The borrower may have to pay these fees based on the following conditions:

1. The loan has a maturity of 15 years or more and the borrower is voluntarily prepaying the loan.

2. The amount to be prepaid is more than 25 percent of the outstanding balance.

3. The prepayment is being made within the first three years after the first disbursement of loan funds.

How the prepayment fee is calculated:

1. First year after disbursement—5 percent of the prepayment amount.

2. Second year after disbursement—3 percent of the prepayment amount.

3. Third year after disbursement—1 percent of the prepayment amount.

SPECIAL-PURPOSE PROGRAMS

The 7(a) program also acts as an umbrella program for several initiatives put into place in order to help businesses with specific circumstances obtain higher guarantees. These initiatives act as incentives for the business world to conform to certain public policy standards or to accomplish certain policy objectives.

These special-purpose loans are geared either toward specific segments of the population or businesses with specific needs. The following programs fall under the 7(a) umbrella and are all subject to annual funding appropriations; as a result, availability may be limited.

- Disabled Assistance Loan (DAL) Program

- 7(a)11 Program

- Solar Energy and Conservation Loan Program

- Export Working Capital Program

- International Trade Loan Program

- Employee Trust Loan Program

- Veterans' Loan Program

- Pollution-Control Loan Program

- Defense Economic Transition Loan Program

- LowDoc Program

- SBAExpress Loan Program

- SBAExport Express Loan Program

- Community Express Loan Program

- CAPLines Loan Program

Disabled Assistance Loan (DAL) Program

Business owners who have a permanent physical, mental, or emotional handicap may qualify for a DAL. This loan was also designed to aid in the funding of nonprofit programs that aid handicapped individuals. This is especially important since, for the most part, nonprofit corporations are ineligible for SBA assistance.

7(a)11 Program

This program helps small businesses to develop in certain urban or rural areas where unemployment is high or where a large number of low-income individuals reside. Businesses operating in these communities are often considered high risk and may have difficulty obtaining traditional funding.

Solar Energy and Conservation Loan Program

In an effort to promote energy conservation, the SBA created the Solar Energy and Conservation Loan Program. This program assists small businesses that design, manufacture, distribute, install, service, or market products or services that help conserve the country's energy resources. It also helps businesses implement alternative energy usage or increase their energy efficiency.

Export Working Capital Program

In order to help small businesses break into the foreign market to sell U.S.-made goods, the SBA provides revolving lines of credit, letters of credit, and other forms of credit through this program.

International Trade Loan Program

This program helps businesses struggling under the weight of import competition that want to pursue international trade opportunities. Because of the size of the international market, the guaranty on loans in this program can be extended to $1.25 million.

Employee Trust Loan Program

Many small businesses use ESOPs (Employee Stock Ownership Programs) as a way to finance growth using internal revenues. This program helps businesses design these and other plans intended to help employees purchase ownership of their employer's business. The cap on SBA assistance for this program is $750,000.

Veterans' Loan Program

Disabled veterans from any era or Vietnam-era veterans can take advantage of this program in order to raise capital for their small businesses.

Pollution-Control Loan Program

In response to the growing environmental threat, the SBA instituted this program to assist businesses that design, plan, install, or build facilities that reduce pollution.

Defense Economic Transition Loan Program

Businesses that suffer due to the closure or reduction of a Department of Defense (DOD) installation can apply for a Defense Economic Transition Loan. This loan also affects both businesses that have had contracts terminated or reduced by the DOD or businesses moving into areas that have been adversely affected by the termination of a DOD program.

LowDoc Program

Very small businesses, often called micro-businesses, may have difficulty obtaining SBA-assisted loans because lenders seldom want to deal with a small loan that is not as profitable and has greater lender risk.

In order to fill this gap in financial availability, the SBA created the LowDoc (low document) program, which reduces the lender's paperwork and offers a 36-hour turnaround time for an SBA decision based on credit scoring tests. These loans are limited to $150,000 maximum.

Although this program does make it easier and faster for the lender, the loan application process for the borrower is not significantly quicker. Not all SBA lenders participate in the LowDoc program.

SBAExpress Loan Program

This fast-track loan program uses the lender's own application forms and approves the loan themselves. The maximum loan is $150,000 with a 50 percent SBA guaranty. In addition to being able to approve the loan, under this program lenders can also approve an unsecured line of credit for as much as $25,000.

SBAExport Express Loan Program

This special SBAExpress loan is geared toward a small business looking to expand or create an export market. Although the maximum loan amount of $150,000 still applies, in this case the SBA will guarantee 85 percent of the loan.

Community Express Loan Program

Another form of the SBAExpress loan, this program is directed toward areas with a high percentage of low-income or unemployed individuals. Also included are areas with a large concentration of SBA new markets (defined as women, Native Americans, Hispanics, Asians, and veterans). The SBA guarantees 50 percent of the loan, with a maximum loan amount of $250,000.

CAPLines Loan Program

This program is designed to help small businesses that need more working capital to grow or whose capital cannot meet the needs of changing seasonal business. These loans are either revolving or non-revolving for as much as $1 million. The SBA will guarantee up to 75 percent of the loan. The five types of CAPLine loans are:

1. **Seasonal credit lines.** For businesses that need to fund increases in inventory and labor due to extreme seasonal or holiday activity.

2. **Contract credit lines.** Used to fund labor and material expenses for one or more of a company's contract jobs.

3. **Builder credit lines.** For building contractors needing financing to cover labor and materials in order to build or renovate homes or commercial properties.

4. **Standard asset-based credit lines.** For small businesses that can't meet the credit requirements for a long-term loan, these revolving lines of credit can help to support increases in inventory or accounts receivables.

5. **Small asset-based credit lines.** For very small businesses that don't qualify even for a standard asset-based credit line, this $200,000 maximum loan has fewer strict servicing requirements.

INELIGIBILITY FOR 7(A) LOANS

Many types of businesses are ineligible for SBA assistance due to the nature of their businesses. These are mostly businesses that involve speculative investment, third-party finance, or passive investments, but also include businesses that engage in unethical or immoral practices.

Businesses that are ineligible for SBA assistance include:

- Those that deal in lewd or pornographic goods or services

- Those that deal with gambling or other illegal activities

- Lenders and investors

- Schools or academies

- Nonprofit corporations and charities

- Those that deal in speculative activities

- Pyramid sales companies

SECTION 504 PROGRAM (CDC LOAN PROGRAM)

Certified Development Companies (CDCs) are nonprofit corporations created to accelerate their community's economic development by providing small businesses with long-term, fixed-rate loans backed by the SBA for the purchase of such major assets as offices or land. These loans cannot be used for:

- Paying off debt

- Restructuring debt

- Working capital

- Inventory

Although the CDC processes the loan applications, the money still comes from SBA-approved lenders. CDCs usually consist of a community of banks, private investors, utilities, and professional organizations, all sharing the risk involved in investing.

Section 504 loans are limited to $1 million in maximum SBA participation. However, if the loan meets a public policy goal, that amount is increased to $1.3 million. These public policy goals can be:

- Expansion of women-owned-and-operated small businesses.

- Expansion of veteran-owned-and-operated small businesses.

- Development of rural areas.

- Minority business development and expansion.

- Development of export market for U.S.-made goods.

- Revitalization of declining business districts.

- Economic competition enhancement.

- Adaptation to federal budget cuts.

Business owners are usually required to sign personal guaranties on the loan and collateral is usually the business's project assets. The term of the loan is usually 10 or 20 years with an interest rate slightly above the current market rate. Also, for every $35,000 provided by the SBA, the business is usually required to either retain or create at least one job.

SBA LOAN DRAWBACKS

The SBA is by no means a perfect entity and, like all forms of funding, does have some negative qualities to consider. Large fees are required of the lender by the SBA in order to guarantee a loan. The lender, in turn, will require reimbursement of this fee from you.

Because the SBA is a government regulatory agency, expect a lot of paperwork and red tape. The SBA will require documentation of everything and will check to make sure the money they guaranteed was spent as intended. If the agency discovers noncompliance, it will cancel the loan and demand immediate repayment.

THE APPLICATION PROCESS

You can approach either an approved lender or the SBA directly to apply for an SBA loan. Either way, you will need to fill out their application forms and provide them with any information they require. Keep your business plan handy and update it if need be.

In order to have even a remote shot at getting your loan approved, you'll have to meet some requirements set down by the lender and the SBA. These include:

- Adequate collateral

- Decent credit record

- Solid management team

- Owner equity (at least 10 percent of the loan's value, invested from your own funds)

- Consistent and adequate cash flow to support loan payments

If you think you have met these requirements, submit your application. Plan on several interviews with the lender, who will contact you and ask you to send your financial information before granting preliminary approval. Make sure you have all of this information together in one place so that you can respond quickly. After your information has been verified by the lender, a loan package will be created and sent to the SBA, which will either approve or reject it. Upon approval, the funding is yours.

SMALL BUSINESS INVESTMENT CORPORATIONS

SBICs are not part of the SBA, but rather privately owned by a community of bankers, investors, and other professionals that acts similarly to venture capitalists. These for-profit organizations are regulated and partially funded by the SBA. They borrow and invest an average of $4 of federal funds for every $1 of private investment money. This, paired with the distribution of investment capital among the members of the SBIC, helps them reduce risk and keep their loan portfolios free of bad loans.

SBICs specialize in equity capital, long-term loans (up to 20 years, with a possible 10-year extension) while providing management assistance to eligible small businesses. Companies that are about to go public and require mezzanine funding are a good match for an SBIC. From the small business owner's perspective, SBICs are a vast source of capital, providing small businesses with $32.7 billion since 1958.

From the investor's perspective, the return on the investment is smaller, usually 20 to 30 percent, but so is the risk. From the SBA's perspective, SBICs help stimulate the small business economy and further public policy goals.

If your business is quite mature or relatively close to going public, SBIC financing might be the way to go. SBICs are generally broken down into three categories:

1. **Traditional SBICs** — Providing loans and debt financing to a wide variety of small businesses.

2. **Specialized SBICs** — Focusing on providing capital for businesses that are owned by the economically or socially disadvantaged.

3. **Venture SBICs** — The most recent incarnation of the SBIC, providing capital to venture capital-eligible firms in order to aid with research and development. This type of SBIC is the one most carefully watched by the SBA.

So if you have a traditional business, such as a retail store or chain of restaurants, the traditional SBIC is the way to go for a loan or for debt financing. If your business is controlled by women or minorities, you may get better terms dealing with a specialized SBIC. If your company is developing a new piece of technology or a drug that is in the public's interest, then a venture SBIC would be your choice.

Obtaining SBIC Funding

The first step in getting SBIC capital is to research the SBICs in your community or in areas crucial to your business. Once you know what is out there, you need to investigate each SBIC thoroughly to see if it would be a good match for your company.

Things to consider when choosing an SBIC:

- Your company's needs

- What types of investments the SBIC makes

- What kind of management services the SBIC offers

- How much money is available

- How much money will be available in the future

- If the time frame is adequate

Planning is crucial. Approach an SBIC as soon as you can project when you will need an infusion of capital. The next step, once you have identified which SBICs are potentially right for your business's needs, is to prepare a presentation and start knocking on doors. Once again, your business plan is the best tool for presenting your business and making a good impression. Make sure it is thorough, complete, and fully updated before approaching an SBIC.

CHAPTER

10

GRANTS

Not much sounds as appealing as "free money" for your business, but be aware that few business ventures are eligible for public or private grant monies. In addition, writing a grant proposal is not for the easily overwhelmed, and, on top of that, few applications are successful.

Before pursuing grant monies, look at one of the U.S. government Web sites listed here. If you believe you have a grant-worthy idea or are opening a nonprofit operation, you need to learn how grants work, what makes an organization eligible, and how to market your idea to the grant committee. Additional resources on grants and grant writing are found in Chapter 19, "Resources."

Typically, direct cash grants are allocated for employee development (recruiting, hiring, and training), for export development for select products or services, or for capital investments to spur community growth. Rarely will you find 100 percent grants from either government agencies or from private charitable foundations; however, there are matching grants (typically a 50 percent match).

There are even some grants that are repaid from future profits with little or no interest. The grant is forgiven if the venture fails. These may be referred to as "seed money" grants.

SEARCHING FOR GRANTS

Finding legitimate grant opportunities can be difficult. Hundreds of people offer grant assistance, grant guides, and "find a grant" Web sites that guarantee success, but these rarely deliver on their promises.

Government grants are available through city, county, state, and federal agencies. Many state and local grants are actually federally funded, so start your research close to home. Contact your local economic development agency and your state's Department of Business and Industry. (Note: Agency names vary from state to state.)

At the centralized U.S. government grant site (**www.grants. gov**), you will find lists of current business grants and specific industry grants. More information may be found at:

- Catalog for Federal Domestic Assistance
  www.cfda.gov

- Small Business Administration grant information
  http://www.sba.gov/expanding/grants.html

- First Gov (the Federal government Web portal)
  http://www.firstgov.gov

- Federal Grant Opportunities
  www.fedgrants.gov

Private Grant Databases and Guides

Most private grant resources are fee-based in which the provider has gathered information from various public sources and resells it to you via Web access, a PDF guide, or a book. However, since grants expire and new ones are launched, beware of copyright dates. Before investing in any grant list, check out the free resources first.

- Fed Money (a grant database operated by a grant software company) at **www.fedmoney.org** has a comprehensive list of government grants and loans. Some services are free; others are fee-based.

Grants for Nonprofits

Not all business ventures are for profit. If your organization is recognized by the Internal Revenue Service as a nonprofit, you will find a greater variety of public and private grants. These grants could be used for such activities as opening a medical clinic in an underserved community, sponsoring research with direct community benefits, or mentoring at-risk teens.

If you are seeking funding for a nonprofit, designate someone in your organization or hire someone to expedite the grant-writing process. Significant funding is related to the grant process.

PRIVATE GRANTS

If you listen to National Public Radio (NPR) or watch Public Broadcasting Service (PBS) stations, you have heard sponsorship messages from privately funded endowments and philanthropic organizations such as the Ford Foundation (**www.fordfound.org**) or the John D. and Catherine T.

MacArthur Foundation (**www.macfound.org**). Such organizations as these are sponsored by corporations, wealthy individuals, and groups interested in human, animal, and community development.

Although most do not provide grants specifically for new business startups, you may find an organization that can provide some financial resources for specific endeavors you hope to undertake. Nonprofit charity, medical research, and new technological advances are the activities most commonly supported by private philanthropic associations.

- The Foundation Center at **www.fdncenter.org** offers updates on numerous private grant programs.

- Check for local or state grants by contacting industry associations, local businesses (ask for their public relations department, as these are often tied in with community visibility) and college/university business departments.

GRANT WRITING ASSISTANCE

Grant writing has its own set of rules and regulations. Nonprofits typically hire a professional grant writer to keep the coffers full. If you are comfortable writing a complete business plan, writing your own grant proposals may be something you would like to undertake. Local universities, community colleges, and business schools frequently offer grant-writing classes. If you are seriously interested in applying for grant funds, this is time and money well-spent.

Hiring a Grant Writer

If you find a significantly large grant (or will seek multiple grants), consider hiring a grant writer, referring to the following guidelines:

1. Determine grant-writing experience and success for organizations similar to yours.

2. Check references carefully.

3. Provide the grant writer with ample information to access the potential for success, provide you with a quote, and match your needs with their skills.

4. Look for a full-time grant writer.

5. Pay an hourly or flat-rate fee (although common, contingency payments can taint the process and may not be in your best interest).

6. Be prepared to work closely together.

7. Review writing samples.

8. If you cannot afford a grant writer to create the entire proposal, seek one who can review and edit your submission.

CAVEAT EMPTOR

Overly optimistic projections, false promises, and even fraudulent activities are not uncommon when you try to obtain grant funds. Beware that your passion and frustration in the money search may color your objectivity. Here are a few things you should remember about obtaining a grant:

- Do not fall for any "Results Guaranteed!" promises.

- Do not pay a finder's fee.

- Verify all grant-related service companies with the Better Business Bureau.

IT TAKES TIME

If you determine that grants are a viable source of financing for your endeavor, build in additional time before you need the money to be in hand. The research process, along with learning how to apply successfully, can take months. Many grants are annual with application deadlines as much as a year away. The review and award time schedules are often many months in advance.

CHAPTER

11 VENTURE CAPITAL

One of the most misunderstood terms in all of finance, venture capital — in its simplest form — is money made available to a growing company by an individual or individuals purchasing ownership in that company.

ABOUT VENTURE CAPITALISTS

Venture capital investing is a fairly new form of business financing. Starting in the 1960s and early 1970s, individual venture capitalists (VCs) began to pool investment monies to jumpstart and grow companies with strong economic potential. With an average fund size of $145 million, venture capital firms now play an important role in growing the U.S. economy. VCs invested more than $21 billion in U.S. companies in 2004 (that's almost twice as much as the SBA financed). Such companies as Apple, Microsoft, Federal Express, and Intel are famous examples of the power of venture capital.

Where Does the Money Come From?

The stereotypical venture capitalist is a wealthy man with tons of cash who controls fates by investing in various businesses. In fact, less than 10 percent of the top-notch VCs are women, and minorities also are underrepresented. However, venture capital investment in minority-owned businesses is growing rapidly and has proven to be quite profitable. Pension plan-funded VCs and public-sector VCs frequently participate in women- and minority-owned VC deals.

Although personal wealth is a universal trait among VCs, these investors have a variety of business and financial experiences, professional backgrounds, and personal interests. As investors, they typically join with like-minded individuals to form a venture capital or equity investment group.

In fact, more than 50 percent of all venture capital investment funds come from public and private pension funds. The balance of VC investments come from endowments, foundations, insurance companies, banks, individuals, and other groups that seek to expand their portfolios into equity investments.

If you seek venture capital, you most likely will work with a professionally managed firm. Contrary to popular belief, VCs are not gamblers blindly trying to catch a wave and cash in on the next trend. Venture capital investments are certainly high risk, but that does not mean VCs do not know what they are doing. VCs, in both the private and public sector, work with advisers (lawyers, accountants, consultants) and are highly connected within multiple industries. Needless to say, they are valuable people to have on your team.

IS VENTURE CAPITAL THE WAY TO GO?

Any newspaper's business section often features the adventures of high-stake investment deals. However, the reality is that few small businesses are suitable candidates for venture capital.

In 2004, when the average per deal was $7.31 million, only 2,873 VC deals were completed. With more than 27 million businesses operating in the United States, this represents a small percentage.

ARE THEY INTERESTED IN YOUR IDEA?

High-dollar investments start with great ideas. Most VC firms are overwhelmed with submissions. Obviously, you must differentiate your business and your product from the crowd.

Big rewards are what motivate VCs. If your idea is not big enough—either in scope or in market share—the potential for exceptional growth and dominance will not be enough to attract aggressive VCs.

Are you a new entrepreneur? VCs look for track records of success (and even failure if you have learned significantly from the venture). Without an exceptional team of professionals, you probably are not a good candidate for VC funding. Are you in an emerging market? Fresh ideas, young markets, and companies with tremendous potential for ongoing new product development are eye-catchers for VC firms.

THE RIGHT MATCH

When seeking an angel investor, partner, or other equity financing, finding the right match for your company is critical. VC firms may invest only in a single industry or in a specific part of the country; some won't work with startups, while others generalize. Generalists look for a broader range of companies and products to fund; however, they still have guidelines you have to meet.

In researching potential VCs, read their guidelines carefully to see if you are a good fit for their investment focus. Your best bet is to start by seeking a VC firm that specializes in your industry. This experience and expertise will provide you with invaluable insight and resources.

The common factor among VC firms is that they are not passive investors, which is both an advantage and a disadvantage. You must be prepared for their active participation and freely given opinions and ideas.

MORE VALUE THAN MONEY

One of the most important benefits of obtaining venture capital is the resource you will find in the VCs themselves. VCs are extraordinarily hard workers, who travel extensively to keep an eye on their various ventures as well as to look out for new ones. They work hard for their money, and they will work hard for you. This is known as a "value-added" investment, where the know-how and support of the investor is often as important as the money invested.

Here are some ways that VCs add value to a growing business:

- Attracting future investors and financial resources.

- Actively participating in strategic development.

- Attending board meetings and providing valuable input.

- Attracting new management team members.

- Providing contacts for potential customers and industry experts.

- Providing access to information previously unavailable to the company.

REWARD VERSUS RISK

Venture capitalists concentrate on balancing reward and risk. Although many will fund startup companies if the forecasted returns seem worth it, most VCs concentrate on more mature companies that are close to going public.

Here are the three most common focuses of venture capital firms:

1. Providing mezzanine funding for companies about to go public.

2. Funding "turnaround" businesses (businesses that are in trouble but have potential for growth).

3. Startups, usually those the investor believes have found a niche or gap in the market, that will produce a high yield.

Many venture capital pools maintain diversity by using a hybrid approach of two or more of these focal points. Because most private investments are illiquid (not immediately convertible to cash), it is important for the investor to occasionally make a safer investment for a more modest return. Safety in investing has become increasingly important to VCs since the dot-com crash of 2000.

STAGES OF FINANCING

Investors will often be heard speaking about stages, phases, or rounds of financing. There are three rounds of financing, with each round usually taking ten years, although some businesses move at a much faster or slower pace.

Some VCs specialize in funding specific stages to dilute the risk, while others will work from startup through the initial public offering (IPO). Over the life of your company, you may work with several VC investors. Before approaching a VC firm, be certain that it works with companies at your firm's growth stage.

Is it better to find one VC for the life of your company? Not necessarily. By working with more than one investment group, you may increase your exposure within the industry through additional PR opportunities, fresh ideas, and new resources.

Like a marriage, a VC relationship will have its ups and downs. Your VC partner may be difficult to work with or not live up to your expectations. These are relationship-based financial arrangements; they require commitment to keep them healthy and flourishing.

THE FIRST ROUND

This round consists of the VC providing seed capital for a startup company with a specific product or service in mind, usually one that fills a gap in the current market.

The VC will fund the first round so that the fledgling company can thoroughly research and develop its product. The seed round contains the most risk, but a successful startup can yield larger returns for the investor who comes into the game early.

During the first and second stages of financing, it is important to take your company's burn rate (how fast it spends investment capital) into consideration. If your company is spending too much too fast, you might find yourself scrambling for additional capital too soon or even going out of business.

Once a successful prototype (also known as an alpha test) of the product is prepared, you are ready to enter the second round of financing.

THE SECOND ROUND

This round, also known as the professional round or first venture round, consists of beta testing the product. Beta testing is the process in which potential customers are given the product, at no cost for a limited time, to use and report their experiences.

While the customers are using it, reported flaws, inconsistencies, or functional limitations can be analyzed. Meanwhile, the business raises capital for marketing the product. A sales-and-marketing strategy is prepared for the eventual release of the product. Once the product is ready to be sold, the third round begins.

THE THIRD ROUND

Commonly referred to as the mezzanine round, the third round is usually the last. Because the business is selling something and making money, additional investments are usually made to allow the company to go public.

The company implements its sales and marketing strategies, hoping eventually to achieve equilibrium between how much money is spent and how much is made. Investors who come late in the game will often pay much more for the security because the investment will become liquid shortly. This liquidity is usually achieved through an IPO, a sale of the entire company to public investors. This is the exit strategy providing the payoff for which you and your investors have been waiting.

FINDING A VENTURE CAPITALIST

The successful VC (the one that can turn $100 million into $300 million, the one you want to attend your board meetings) has enough contacts to avoid looking through the "slush pile" of thousands of business plans mailed to his office. Do not waste time cold-calling venture capital firms.

There are three ways to find a VC:

1. Make it find you.

2. Be introduced.

3. Find seekers.

Make It Find You

Don't look for venture capital; make it come looking for you. Here are some common ways VCs discover moneymaking opportunities:

- Advisory boards consisting of specialists in individual industries, tracking trends, and finding gaps in the market.

- Keeping a watchful eye on managers and entrepreneurs who have had success in the past.

- Maintaining relationships with research institutions and the academic world, where a lot of important research happens.

- Inventing companies themselves by recognizing gaps in the market and building a company to fill the needs of the market, piece by piece.

- Waiting for a company to establish itself, and then providing mezzanine funding before the company's IPO.

Get Introduced to VCs

If you are not yet completely disheartened at the thought of trying to obtain venture capital, and are serious about landing a deal, here are some steps to take in order to gain access to a VC:

- **Arranging an introduction** — It is not uncommon for entrepreneurs to hire consultants who specialize in venture capital. This is because these specialists know venture capitalists and can introduce you to them. Usually, VCs rely on a few consultants they trust, including lawyers, accountants, and special placement agencies, to bring them promising deals.

- **Ask around** — It is also important to ask the people around you. Do you happen to know anyone who knows a VC and could introduce you? Your accountant? Your lawyer? Maybe someone on your board of directors or advisory board knows a VC. It doesn't hurt to ask. Actually, it could help quite a bit.

- **Event attendance** — Attend conferences, luncheons, business fairs, charity events, etc. Search the Web for local event-sponsoring organizations. VCs frequent these events to keep their finger on the pulse of the business world.

- **Media coverage** — Invite local papers and magazines to write about your company. Provide information about what is interesting or special about your business and your products. If you do not have a public relations background, hire a professional. PR people are expensive to have on staff, but they are invaluable to a growing business.

Find a Seeker

There are some VC groups that are seekers, meaning they actively look for investment proposals. These are typically smaller groups, often specializing within niche markets or less well-known industries. Some have a social or political agenda. Use caution in responding to advertisements and Web sites looking for businesses needing venture capital funds.

MONEY FOR MINORITIES

Often businesses with socially relevant products (ecologically friendly or innovative) and women- and minority-owned companies are informally allocated a percentage of investment funds from VCs. Some VCs specialize in financing these minority enterprises.

Minority investments are profitable. The average investment being $562,000 per firm with a gross yield per firm of $1,623,900. Minority-oriented venture capital funds do not concentrate on high-tech ventures. Public pension funds are the main source of VC funds for minority businesses.

WHAT TO AVOID IN A VENTURE CAPITALIST

No matter how badly your business needs the capital, it is not worth the potential loss to work with VCs who display the following traits:

- **Inexperience** — Earning an MBA or having a few years of Wall Street experience does not make an effective venture capitalist. It is the experience of bringing businesses through many rounds of funding and ultimately to a public offering that makes a VC worth pursuing. Make sure the VC has serious hands-on experience and is not merely focused on a quick return.

- **Poor reputation** — Do your homework when researching VCs. Know where the other businesses in their portfolio stand, and avoid VCs who have backed a substantial number of businesses that have not met projections. Also, check to see if they are known for replacing the founders of companies.

- **Poor attitude** — Entrepreneurs should make sure that the VC does not have an aloof attitude toward the business. The communication lines should remain open between the investor and the founder. The founder should be able to contact the VC personally. Also, it is important that the VC understands that you run the business.

- **Overcommitted** — Some VCs take on more than they can handle, promising to guide and direct your business while simultaneously serving on the board of other startup companies, all the while trying to organize a new fund.

- **Takes advantage** — Avoid the VC who tries to exploit your early-stage business when the market is down by demanding insane terms and large share price decreases.

Talk to the CEOs of the VC's prior investments. Talk to those who head successful investments, but also talk with the ones who didn't make it or faired only so-so. This sort of insight will be useful when trying to determine the character of the VC. For venture capital trade organizations and associations, see Chapter 19, "Resources."

ASKING QUESTIONS

VCs are willing to invest more than money when they consider a deal — they are accepting an enormous amount of responsibility and accountability for the success of your company. Expect to be thoroughly questioned about the particulars of your business. They want to evaluate you along with your management team to determine if entrusting you is a wise decision.

The interview process can be unnerving, but do not be afraid to assert yourself and ask some questions afterward. Even if they are not interested in making a deal, this is an opportunity to learn from an experienced group of investors. Ask questions and be prepared for candid answers.

- What did you think of the business plan? What modifications would you make?

- How could we improve the management team?

- If you were to invest "x" dollars, what do you think a fair market share value would be for the business?

- Do you think we have an accurate picture of the market? the competition?

- In what ways is business vulnerable to competition?

- How will existing competition react to our presence in the market?

- Is our time frame feasible? Can we achieve our business goals in the time allotted?

Their answers will reveal a great deal about the kind of investors they are. You will be able to tell not only if they have done their homework but also whether they are seriously considering the proposal. You will get a glimpse into the character of these investors, which will help you decide if you want to be in business with them. In addition, you will make a good impression by asking questions. VCs will see that you are confident enough in your venture to be receptive to criticism.

THE LONG ROAD TO OBTAINING VENTURE CAPITAL

In many ways, obtaining venture capital is just like anything else in business. Plan well, adapt, and work extremely hard and eventually you will get there. However, to lend some focus to the search, a general overview might be useful:

Begin with an Idea

Start with an idea that has commercial appeal. It does not have to be a high-tech concept or overly complicated. Just be certain that there is a receptive market for your idea.

Without much capital or many resources, you must do the research to determine whether it can be accomplished by a startup venture. No matter how terrific your idea, if there is no market, then it is best to table it.

Write a Business Plan

Put everything on paper, even if it is only for your own reference. You will find an overview on writing a business plan in Chapter 3 and additional resources in Chapter 19.

Find Seed Capital

Whether you use personal assets or borrow money from a bank, friend, or family member, it is imperative that you begin without financing from a VC. This experience will provide you with invaluable information about your abilities as a manager as well as about your customers, your competitors, and the marketplace.

If you feel uncomfortable with this advice, remember the dot-com startups funded by VCs in 1999, and how most ended up taking a dive. Many entrepreneurs that are funded by VCs in the seed round wish they had been on their own for the first few years.

Once your business is established, you can negotiate better terms as well. After all, venture capitalists are often called "vulture capitalists" for their reputation of wanting too much equity for too little money.

Build a Prototype and Beta Test It

Discover whether your product really does what you thought it would. Offer free trials to potential customers, and listen carefully to their feedback. Now is the time to fine-tune your product. Make sure the product you put on the market is as perfect as it possibly can be. Begin planning for future versions of the product or upgrades of the technology.

Modify Your Plan

Carefully consider and adapt to the feedback you receive from the beta test. Make the modifications that may determine whether or not your product sells. Update your business plan.

Consider how much money you have spent versus how much you projected to spend. Make a thorough revision of your business plan as you prepare to present it to potential investors. Businesses that can adapt are businesses that attract venture capital.

In addition, concentrate on writing a solid marketing plan to attract customers. Update your strategies based on the customers' responses to the beta test, or you may end up with a warehouse full of product.

Sell Your Product, Build the Company

The real challenge begins when you start marketing the product to customers. Test, explore, and target potential customers. Revise your strategy and try again. Develop a consistent, trusted brand and image.

Consider another round of financing. Many entrepreneurs pursue angel investors at this stage; this can be a wise move. The funding received from angels, usually from $500,000 to $3 million, should be allocated for marketing and distribution and for adding key members to your management team.

Venture Capital, Finally

VCs will look at your management team to see if you've hired capable, talented, and dependable professionals. If you have built a solid team, developed a product with purpose, and served your customers well, a VC will likely approach you. Further encourage them by attending conferences, obtaining write-ups in the newspaper, and working to gain an introduction.

When you meet with a venture capital firm, be sure they give your company a fair valuation. By this point, you should know what your business is worth, so insist on a fair and accurate valuation. Entrepreneurs who let investors bully them end up with little equity when it is time to cash out.

CHAPTER

12 Angel Investors

T he business equivalent of a miracle worker is an angel investor. Angels are individuals or small investment groups that invest directly into private startup businesses. Angels invest smaller amounts than venture capitalists, but they tolerate an equally high risk; hence, they expect significant returns.

WHO ARE ANGELS?

Angels are a fascinating and diverse breed of investor. They range from retired CEOs looking to share their years of wisdom to recently wealthy young entrepreneurs who want to stay in the game. Some band together for common goals, while others prefer to go it alone. Many rely on chance encounters to discover deals, but a growing segment of the angel population looks for opportunities.

Angels are an important source of funding for many startup and early-stage business ventures. When you have a marketable product and need seed capital, an angel may be your salvation. Like venture capitalists, angels are often willing to take a risk on investing in new technology or unproven business concepts. Unlike VCs, however, angels will usually invest earlier in the game without demanding as high of a return. Also, angels invest their own money rather than other people's funds.

Angels know the risks of investing in early-stage companies and accept those risks. Although their motivations are as diverse as their backgrounds, most angels agree that they are in it for more than the money.

THE EQUITY CHOICE

Angels fill a gap between big-bucks venture capitalists and acquaintance investors. Their investment of more than $10,000 and less than $1 million is more than most families or friends can supply, but smaller than what most venture capital firms or investment banks prefer to invest. Loans are available in this range; however, equity financing may be a wiser choice for your business. Chapter 8 explores debt versus equity financing.

ANGEL SUPPORT

Although the money an angel brings to the business is crucial, the angel's advice and vision can also play a central role in the company's success. Angels are experienced and successful businesspeople. Whether they earned their fortunes as corporate executives, entrepreneurs, or through inherited wealth, they offer valuable insights, ideas, and support. Angels also introduce other angels and potential customers.

Angels may seem like the perfect solution for a small business needing early growth capital, but angels are not as easy to locate as it might seem. The 1990s dot-com crash caused many heavily invested high-tech angels to become skeptical of high-risk, high-return opportunities. As a result, many angels are rethinking their investing styles, researching more diligently, and investing more conservatively.

EXPLORING THE TYPES OF ANGELS

Before the dot-com crash, the 2000 stock market escalation created trillions of dollars of new money for entrepreneurs and investors alike. This newly created wealth not only increased the number of angels looking for high-return investment opportunities, but this wealth also redefined what an angel was or could be.

Suddenly, not only retired CEOs or investment bankers were angels; eager young entrepreneurs, particularly those in the technology industry who struck it rich, were becoming angels. These newly minted millionaire investors brought both fresh enthusiasm to the world of angel investing as well as a great deal of technical expertise. Having made their fortunes almost overnight, they were accustomed to innovative, high-risk ventures, enjoying accelerated double- (and even triple-) digit returns.

However, when things started to decline for the dot-coms and other technology-based industries, many of these new investors watched their wealth diminish as quickly as it was created. This sudden drop convinced many that angel investing was not for them. Experienced angels, or core angels, accepted the loss as a minor setback—something they had faced before and would face again.

The wisest angels view a downturn as a positive event that allows them to get good deals on ownership because valuations are so low. In addition, the competition for these deals is significantly reduced as the less experienced angels wait out the market.

ANGELS, GENERALLY SPEAKING

Angels are found in three broad categories. Within each of these categories are subgroups with specific investor characteristics. Many angels have specific emotional needs that they fulfill through hands-on investing activities.

The Core Angel

The most experienced type, the core, or serial, angel has been through the process of investing and harvesting (cashing out) on many occasions. In this sense, he or she can be a valuable asset to any startup or early-stage company by working as an adviser or mentor.

Core angels typically keep a diverse portfolio of public and private stock as well as real estate. Core angels are dedicated to their investments, so the entrepreneur should not worry about them backing out of an agreement.

The Tech Angel

Tech angels are usually younger, less experienced angels who have an enthusiasm for bringing new technologies to the market. Although they may not have as much investment experience, they do possess a good working knowledge of technology. These angels make smart investments and can guide young technology companies to success. They are enthusiastic risk-takers who help new technologies get to market.

The Silent Angel

These angels are primarily interested in a big return on their investment. These angels will invest based on their perceptions of what their peer angels are earning. They often consider an investment to be a diversification in their portfolio and care little about the day-to-day operations of the business. Silent angels will not provide any advice, wisdom, or mentoring.

Some questions to ask about prospective angels:

- How involved do I want the angel to be?

- How much of my company's ownership am I willing to surrender?

- Does my angel have the background or technological know-how to understand my business?

- Can this angel introduce me to other angels or venture capitalists?

- Does this angel have the patience required?

OTHER ANGELS

Recognizing other angels will help you decide whether or not a particular angel is right for your business.

- **Mentor angels** — These angels are the true angels, believing that their experience is more important than the money they invest. They act as advocates for the business and have a genuine interest in the day-to-day operations. They are invaluable to early-stage businesses, as both consultants and encouragers.

- **Leader angels** pride themselves both on discovering deals and on bringing other angels and investors to the table. They are natural salespeople and valuable assets if you plan on more rounds of financing.

- **Underhanded, or dark, angels** exhibit the dark side of angel investing. These angels invest with the specific intention of muscling out the founders and taking over once the business has become successful.

- **Grandfather angels** usually head large bands of angels and have been angel investing for a long time. They are powerful and influential.

- **Inheritance angels** usually use family money, trying to make it grow. They can be skilled business executives or they may have no business or financial experience whatsoever.

- **Newcomer angels** — Recently wealthy and tentative, these angels often invest together to share the risk. Few of these angels reach the status of a full-fledged angel.

- **Do-gooder angels** — Social responsibility is at the forefront of these angels' list of objectives. Of course they want to make money, but they are interested only in companies that have what is known as a "double bottom line." They fund companies engaged in everything from community development to cancer research.

- **Moonlighting angels** are venture capitalists by day, angels by night. These VCs take advantage of deals that are either too small or unsuited for their VC firm. Some venture capital firms frown on this practice, but others encourage it, believing it keeps their VCs sharp.

- **Even-exchange angels**, also known as work-for-equity angels or sweat-equity angels, provide a needed service in exchange for a portion of the business's equity. These are usually Web-design firms, marketing firms, or PR firms. Although it may seem like a good idea, make sure you know how much your equity is worth before agreeing to such an arrangement; it might be less costly to simply cut them a check for their services.

RECENT ANGEL TRENDS

To see where angel investing is headed, it is necessary to look at where it has been. Of course, it is impossible to predict what will happen in the private-equity market, but a look back can help us learn.

The Dot-Com Boom

The years of 1999 and 2000 saw more investing in a short time that the private-equity market had ever witnessed. Anything to do with the Internet seemed to get instant funding, largely because Web site values were based on the number of visitors received rather than on the revenue generated.

Admittedly, this was a ridiculous business model. The overvaluations of these businesses were more ridiculous. Many investors, who should have known better, fell for the allure of the Internet frenzy and were afraid of being left behind and missing out on the excitement and fast cash. When it became clear that many of these Internet ventures were failures, investors were shocked back to their senses. By 2001, the slow-and-steady business model was back in place, and many would-be angels dropped out of the investment world for good.

In light of this downturn, entrepreneurs began to lose heart. Many simply gave up the search for capital. This correction in the investment world did not mean funding was unavailable. In fact, serious angel investors believe the current climate is perfect for investing. There is less competition for good deals and valuations are lower, making equity more affordable.

True angels know that just because the market drops does not mean there are not opportunities in the market or that people stop generating ideas to fill consumer needs. Angels are, however, exercising more caution, which means you have to be more attractive, better prepared, and more creative.

In many ways angels resemble venture capitalists. As angels demand more rigid guidelines, business plans, and greater control over investments, the line between VC and angel is beginning to blur.

Getting Back on Track

Even angels who stopped making new investments to cultivate existing investments will resume investing. Once their existing investments show signs of upward movement, angels will face new investments with as much enthusiasm as before.

ANGELS' CHALLENGES

Being an angel is not easy, and knowing what challenges face angels is important to an entrepreneur looking for angel capital. Anything an entrepreneur can do to make the angel's life easier will ultimately improve the chances of raising capital.

From the Angel's Perspective

Looking at things from the angel's perspective will help you find an angel and interest him or her in your venture. Know what traits they look for in management as well as what deals they select and what deals they forgo.

How Angels Find Deals

The angel perspective on finding a deal varies. More aggressive angels use multiple methods, including networking, joining an angel band, keeping in contact with old business connections, even becoming an active member of their alma mater's alumni association. However, the primary way angels connect with entrepreneurs is through referrals.

With that in mind, tell your business associates, peers, family, and friends that you are looking for an angel investor. Participation in trade associations, conventions, community economic development seminars, and entrepreneur-oriented clubs is another good way to get out the word. The Internet is yet another valuable resource for connecting investors and entrepreneurs.

The Web has opened a whole new resource for startups; however, be aware that the potential for fraud and misrepresentation has also increased. The ability to meet someone face to face and discuss your business concept continues to be a critical part of the decision-making process. It is best to deal with local angel; however, that may not be possible depending upon your needs and industry.

Beware of:

1. **Guaranteed money.** Money brokers often "guarantee" they will find you an investor.

2. **Finder's fees.** Avoid these up-front fees. There are legitimate consultants who provide valuable services, but unless you can verify their legitimacy, you will have little recourse should they fail to deliver. Instead, negotiate fees based upon money raised or other services that can be measured as successful.

3. **Incomplete references.** Check with satisfied and not-so-satisfied clients.

4. **Not accredited.** Verify that your investor is accredited as defined by the Securities and Exchange Commission (SEC) in Rule 501 of Regulation D.

If you use the Internet, a great place to start searching for angel investors is through the SBA and other legitimate associations. You can find angel investor resources in Chapter 19.

ACTIVE CAPITAL—THE SBA CONNECTION

In the mid 1990s, the SBA created ACE-Net as a way to foster better access for small businesses to private capital. Now operating as Active Capital at **www.activecapital.org**, businesses may apply to be listed in their "seeking funding" database. This national database is available for accredited investors to review your needs and find complementary goals.

Companies seeking investors through Active Capital and the ACE-Net database system must submit a confidential application. As of September 2005, qualified businesses must have a registered or qualified securities offering under federal securities Regulation A (up to $5 million) or Regulation D (up to $1 million) and corresponding state security regulations.

In addition to acting as a go-between, nonprofit Active Capital provides training and counseling to help entrepreneurs in attracting angel investors.

DECIDING WHICH DEALS ARE RIGHT

An angel is not a venture capitalist, so the angel process of due diligence is less formal than that of their VC counterparts. Nevertheless, a wise angel will have strong business and industry experience and will listen carefully.

The Internet has vastly improved the flow of available information, making the arduous task of due diligence more simplified. Angels understand that instinct will take them only so far; using the Internet has expedited the decision-making process.

Risk management is another factor angels must constantly consider. They must decide if there is room in their portfolio for a high-risk venture or if they need to balance existing high-risk investments with lower-risk companies.

Deciding How Much Assistance to Give

Although the angel knows you want his advice and support, he has to decide how much guidance to give. Your angel has a substantial sum of money invested in your company, which gives him the right to speak up as needed.

So how to achieve this delicate balance? Through trust. The angel knows that he has invested in your company and your management team because he thought you were capable of leading the company. The entrepreneur must also trust that the angel has the best interests of the company in mind when he gives advice or suggests a direction the company should take.

ATTRACTING ANGEL INVESTORS

Understand, of course, that each angel is an individual and should be dealt with as such. Discussing them as a group, however, can make approaching them (or getting them to approach you) much easier.

What Angels Want

The level of rejection entrepreneurs face from investors, especially venture capitalists, is staggering. A common mistake by many young founders is to simply give up looking for capital because the perceived amount of rejection indicates that their venture is not feasible. What these founders may not realize is they probably didn't match the investor's criteria. Chances are good that the proposal never made it through the initial screening process. This hardly can be considered rejection, if the venture was never considered in the first place. The need for early-stage growth or seed capital eliminates many proposals immediately. Angel investors, on the other hand, are quite fond of early-stage ventures and believe they will be well compensated for the risks.

It should be noted that angels do have individual preferences. Entrepreneurs must do the research to find out which angels are suited to the venture. Once again, word-of-mouth is a great way to find the right angel for you.

Possible angel investment criteria:

- **Geography** — Angels prefer to work locally, so they can keep abreast of the business. Also, networking with friends and associates is a great way for angels to find the best deals.

- **Industry** — Angels prefer to invest in what they know in order to better fulfill their advisory role in the new business.

- **Investment size** — Some angels are more comfortable with large investments than others. Some have more money to invest. For the most part, angels deal in smaller investments than large banks and VCs.

Once you have researched the angels in your area and figured out which ones are candidates for your business, you can begin to make contact.

Making Contact

Seeking an angel may seem daunting, but there are tried-and-true methods for meeting angels that have worked for many small businesses.

The basic ways of attracting angels are as follows:

- Networking

- Media attention

- Events

- Angel lists

- Internet matching services

- Referrals

Networking

Networking is one of the most valuable things you can do for your business, whether or not you are currently seeking to raise capital. Word-of-mouth has long been held as the best kind of advertisement available.

Getting out of the office to network and socialize can be difficult at times, particularly when it seems that all of your time and energy need to be devoted to working. Remember, though, going out and chatting up your venture while playing a few rounds of golf, for instance, can be even more productive than sitting in your desk chair.

Talk to your friends about your desire to implement your idea. Tell your lawyer about it, your doctor, your personal trainer, whoever. After all, they might know an angel.

Talk to people about your venture, but don't bore them. Over-explaining can turn off people both to your idea and to you. Be confident, but be subtle as well.

Media Attention

Because angel investors like to work locally, they keep an eye on the local news for possible investment opportunities. If there is a chance for your company to make a headline or two, take it. Attracting an angel this way can save a lot of headaches. Chances are good that if they take the time to contact you, they are confident that they are well-suited for your business.

Keep in mind that there are laws concerning "general advertising and soliciting" when seeking investors. Consult with a PR specialist and with your lawyer before embarking on a media blitz.

Events

Event attendance can be crucial for finding an angel. Angels regularly attend conferences and presentations in order to stay abreast of the current market climate and to meet new business contacts.

Consider joining your local chamber of commerce. In addition, such organizations as the Elks Club, Lions Club, and Rotary Club are great places to meet angels.

Venture capital clubs frequently meet to provide entrepreneurs with a forum for presenting their business ideas. These clubs exist all over the United States in more than 100 different locations. If there is one near you, become an active participant.

Angel Lists

Lists of angels, although far from complete, are a good place to start looking. Many universities, economic development agencies, SCORE, and entrepreneur clubs have created lists. The local library is also sure to have books containing the names and contact information for literally hundreds of angels and angel bands.

Internet Matching Services

There are many Internet matching services available that will, for a fee, attempt to match your business with a like-minded angel. This is an option to consider, but do not expect it to immediately deliver an angel to your doorstep.

Referrals

Most businesspeople no doubt have a Rolodex full of business cards collected over the years from vendors, customers, old college friends, and others. These are not only phone numbers, but they also are a valuable source of potential capital, as CrystalView, Inc. of Waltham, Massachusetts, a supplier of automated home care equipment, found out.

When CrystalView needed $2 million in seed capital, President Bruce Nappi put together an offering and sent it to 400 potential investors, all found within his Rolodex. His original list turned up six investors as well as a new list of 80 more names, all referred to him by his original contacts.

This new list of names turned up eight more investors, and CrystalView then had $250,000 of its $2 million goal. One of the referrals did not invest, but instead helped the company refine its business plan and provided another list of potential investors, which generated five more investors.

Nappi then gave a 15-minute presentation with three other capital-seekers at a venture capital forum. Although the audience response was positive, it did not generate a single investor. However, Nappi swapped leads with the other three presenters, and from these he managed to secure the rest of CrystalView's $625,000 minimum for the deal.

Nappi notes that only five percent of the leads he spoke to on the phone wanted to look at the business plan, but half of those led to a personal meeting. Because all of these contacts were personal referrals, Nappi was not pushy, electing instead to be gentle, not endangering the new relationships. As a rule, investors that are genuinely interested in a deal will close it quickly. Initially reluctant investors rarely invest at all.

Beginning with a strong list of potential investors is a wonderful thing. As CrystalView now knows, the referrals that the list generates are as valuable as the original list.

When contacting potential investors, remember to ask if they know of anyone who might be interested in your deal. Expanding your list of contacts by using a referral lends context to your solicitation.

Investors usually will only refer you to people they know and trust, so you can confidently use their relationships as foundations for your own new relationships.

Remember that angels who choose not to invest can help in other ways besides referrals. They may have valuable insights on ways to improve your pitch or your business plan. You should not hesitate to ask them why they are not interested in investing.

WHAT ANGELS LOOK FOR IN ENTREPRENEURS

Successful entrepreneurs need to have a myriad of skills, and angels look for evidence of those skills and talents when making a deal. Here is a list of those traits that are most attractive to angel investors:

- Drive and passion

- Vision

- Commitment

- Honesty and integrity

- Willingness to learn

- Adaptability

- Open-mindedness

- Experience

- Industry-specific knowledge

- Ability to build an excellent team

- Self-discipline

- Foresight

- Network of contacts

- Patience

- Communication skills

- Cooperation

Individual angels will evaluate you according to their own set of standards. Do your best to embody as many of the above characteristics as possible.

Angel investors look not only for products that will make them money, but also for people. They consider themselves to be making as much of an investment in you as they are in your company or technology.

Angels will ruthlessly scrutinize your management team and may only fund you on the condition that you bring in new talent; often they have someone specific in mind. Angels want to make money, and they understand that your management team is who will ultimately make it for them.

When you finally meet with an angel, present your idea in as many different ways as possible. Provide visual as well as written presentations, as many people relate better to either one or the other. And, contrary to popular belief, angels will read your business plan.

13 INITIAL PUBLIC OFFERINGS

Initial public offerings (IPOs) are a popular exit strategy for investors and founders alike. They are the realization of every entrepreneur's dream—the big payoff, the culminating achievement. Most simply, though, an IPO is another way to raise capital.

An IPO consists of turning private ownership stakes into publicly traded stocks by selling them on the stock market. The equity of the business then becomes liquid, thereby raising cash with every stock sold. If all goes well, the cash raised can be hundreds of millions of dollars.

IPOs were once only for mature businesses with proven records of success. As more people made investing in the public arena a career, young businesses started to move to the IPO stage, even before generating a profit. The idea behind this is simple and reminiscent of many investors' dream of getting in on the ground floor and reaping high returns. The public became accustomed to buying stock from a company with no proven track record, believing the stock price would skyrocket. The phenomenon of buying stock from companies that are valued low and hoping the stock will miraculously go up seems to have dwindled thanks to the crash of the dot-com industry. Nevertheless, small businesses make IPOs all the time.

Having cash resources to grow your business sounds like a dream come true, but you must consider the question, "Will it help or hurt my business?"

THE BIG DECISION

Founders need to carefully consider whether or not the time is right to make an IPO. Market conditions change constantly, and waiting for a period that is favorable to IPOs is crucial.

Many entrepreneurs push their business into an IPO simply because they can even though a different source of financing would have made more sense. An IPO requires a great deal of work on the part of the entrepreneur and the management team, so it must be considered carefully.

Weigh the following factors before committing to an IPO:

- Can your company's reputation withstand a failed IPO?

- Does the money you make cover the sweat equity you have put into the firm?

- Is your firm prepared for the serious long-range consequences that result from becoming a public company?

- Are other alternatives to financing the company worth considering?

- Knowing the size and growth ability of your company, will it generate interest and sell stock?

BENEFITS AND DRAWBACKS

Obviously an IPO has both pros and cons. Carefully consider the positives and negatives of the equation before making your decision.

Benefits

Raising capital at an almost unprecedented rate is and will always be the main benefit of an IPO. However, there are a few other reasons going public can work for you besides a better price for your stock shares, including the following:

- Increased liquidity for investors, founders, and venture capitalists. Investors can buy and sell stocks more easily. Founders and owners can eliminate personal guarantees. Owners can more easily exit the business. Stockholders can diversify, eliminating estate tax issues.

- Improved employee compensation. Stock and stock options can be used to attract and reward talented employees. Performance bonuses can also incorporate stock.

- Enhanced recognition and greater level of respectability and perceived stability. Customers and suppliers feel more comfortable when dealing with a public entity.

- Generated publicity and increased visibility beyond your industry.

- Established value and increased potential for mergers and acquisitions.

- Enhanced net worth for shareholders. Can be easily converted to cash or used as collateral to secure loans.

- Ability to easily raise cash again through stock offerings.

Drawbacks

The challenges of making a company public frequently outnumber the benefits, depending on the situation. Carefully consider the following before making the final decision about proceeding with an IPO:

- All of your company's information is disclosed to the public. Your holdings, pricing strategies, profits, and compensations are available.

- Profits must be shared with outsiders. A typical IPO leaves about 40 percent of the company ownership with insiders. However, this figure (depending upon the industry) can range from 20 to 60 percent.

- In the time it takes to file an IPO and for the SEC to reach a decision (up to six months), market conditions may have changed and the IPO window may have closed. It might stay closed for several years. If you were counting on the money the IPO was going to generate, you might be forced into bankruptcy.

- The costs of transitioning from a private to public company can be enormous. Underwriters usually receive as much as 15 percent right off the bat, and another 10 to 15 percent will go toward accounting, printing, and legal costs. So if your IPO is $5 million, up to $1,250,000 could be gone by the time the company gets anything. During the first half of 2005, average out-of-pocket IPO expenses were $3,394,334 per company. IPO legal fees during that same period averaged $1,076,534 and auditor fees averaged $701,530.

- Lockups often prevent founders and other insiders from selling their stock during and after an IPO. Overcoming these restrictions can be quite a difficult.

- Increased liability as mandated by the Private Securities Litigation Reform Act of 1995 under which IPO participants are jointly and severally liable for each others' actions.

- Extensive reporting requirement and increased financial responsibilities. Federal SEC and state security laws require constant disclosure, standardized recordkeeping, and regular filings.

PAPERWORK

Over the past few decades, many new legal requirements have been put into place to closely regulate public companies and prevent insider trading. These are numerous and tedious, and not abiding by them can get you and the company into serious legal trouble. The major requirements to consider include:

- Quarterly and annual reports that must be filed to the SEC, as well as so-called flash reports that must be filed immediately when any significant business move is made. This publication of short-term results can hurt the image of the company by not representing what it is capable of in the long term.

- The public must receive reports every day, and at the same time as analysts and investment firms. These disclosure laws are part of Regulation FD, passed in 2000 by the SEC.

- Annual meetings now require a great deal of work, and the disclosure emphasis is mostly on what management is paid. If analysts think management is paid too much or too little, they see this as a sign of poor corporate performance. Frustratingly, management compensation is seldom cited by private analysts as an important factor in determining a company's performance.

There are many more IPO-triggered regulations, too numerous to list here. It is important to consult with a lawyer who has been through the IPO process before and knows where the pitfalls are and how to step around them.

Think seriously about the consequences of opening your company to the public. If there is evidence of any business practice that the public might interpret as unethical, your IPO could turn into an embarrassing and costly event.

IPO PREPARATION

If, after careful analysis, you decide that now is the time for an IPO, you will need to know the process. Preparing fully is the best way to ensure that your IPO goes as smoothly as it possibly can. By combining timing, preparation, skill, and a little luck, you increase your chances of being one of the few businesses that really clean up on IPOs each year.

Putting the IPO Team Together

No founder should take on the task of making an IPO alone. You will need help, especially if this is your first experience in taking a business public. The more experienced the team, the better your chances of success. Make sure you are surrounded by experts with good reputations and experience in handling the paperwork and forms that the IPO demands.

The IPO team should consist of, at the very least:

1. **Your management team** including you, the CEO, the CFO, the COO, and marketing managers.

2. **A specialist PR firm** that primarily handles businesses that go public. Plan to change PR firms at this point, if your current one does not have this experience.

3. **Lawyers with substantial IPO experience.** They must have a thorough understanding of the complicated laws and regulations involved with going public.

4. **Accountants** who know your industry and deal primarily with public companies in that industry.

5. **A well-respected investment bank** with a high profile. Make sure they have a good track record in your specific industry.

Since you and your IPO team will be spending the next six months or so working closely together, make sure that everyone gets along. Clashing personalities or ideals can make a stressful situation even more so. Hold interviews with a multitude of individuals and firms.

Building your team usually takes two to three months before the filing of the IPO. You might have to convince certain members of your team that now is the right time to go for the IPO. Make sure you have the backing of your team before proceeding. If your team members waver, consider that backing out early is far preferable to backing out late. Even backing out late is preferable to having your IPO crash.

If you have your team's consensus, and everyone decides that now is the time to go for it, start an audit. This audit will take an additional two to three months, but it is vital to the process. You cannot file for the IPO without it.

Generally Accepted Accounting Principles

Chances are good that, unless you are a very small company, you already do this, and there is certainly no point in changing your accounting system now. In fact, changing methods can cause worry in the minds of investors, who might see it as a sign that you are trying to hide something.

You have also probably had your company's finances audited by an independent CPA firm. This means, essentially, that you have everything you need, financially speaking, ready to go for the IPO.

If this is the first time, though, that your company is being audited independently, now would be an excellent time to set your records straight and start keeping track of finances according to generally accepted accounting principles (GAAP).

Correctly and completely prepared financial documentation eases the IPO process tremendously. If your IPO is still many years off, seriously consider conforming your records to GAAP standards now, in order to save time in the future.

Forms

Submitting the appropriate forms is the next step in the process of moving toward an IPO. These forms are for the SEC to approve. Without SEC approval, it is pointless to move forward with the IPO. Your lawyers, backed by the other members of your team, will be the ones actually filling out these forms.

Accompanying these forms is the prospectus, discussed in detail later, and any other pertinent supplemental information required by the SEC, including a cost breakdown of the expenses incurred while making your initial public offering.

There are a few options as far as what registration form to use; your lawyer will know which is right for your company. The form requirement usually depends on the size of your business.

S-1

No matter what the size of your company, you can always use the S-1 form to register for an IPO. Because it is widely available to any size business, it is naturally the most comprehensive and complicated of all the forms.

If your business can fill out an alternative form, it might save you some serious time. The S-1 asks you to outline the following information in your prospectus:

- Nature of the business.

- Properties of the business.

- Names of management and key players, and their compensation packages.

- Industry competition.

- Documentation of litigation that has involved the company or any of its key players.

- Transactions involving the company and its board or officers.

- What the money from the IPO is going to be used for and how securities will be publicly distributed.

- Risk factors, including industry's economic status, unproven operating history, and reliance on specific personnel.

- Supporting information delivered to the SEC, including three years worth of SEC-approved audited financial statements.

SB-1

A question-and-answer style form that is designed specifically for small businesses as an alternative to the bulky S-1. It is more user friendly, taking far less time to complete than the S-1. You must meet certain standards, however, to be considered eligible for this form, including the following:

- Less than $25 million in revenues last fiscal year.

- Outstanding publicly held stock totaling $25 million or less.

- Securities offered must be no more than $10 million in any one year.

Accompanying this form should be at least two years' worth of audited financial statements meeting GAAP standards.

SB-2

The SB-2 is another alternative to the S-1, again for small businesses adhering to the same standards as the SB-1. However, in this case, the dollar amount of registered securities is unlimited. The same requirement of two years' audited financial statements meeting GAAP standards applies.

Preliminary Pricing

Pending approval of the SEC, the founder and his or her team should begin to think about pricing the IPO. This preliminary pricing is dependant on a number of factors, namely:

- How much money is to be raised?

- How many shares are expected to be sold?

- Market conditions.

- Stock prices of comparable public companies.

- Number of shares outstanding before the IPO.

- Valuation of the company.

A basic way to think about pricing the IPO is to begin with the amount of money you wish to raise, say $30 million. If a reasonable target price per share is $10, then the offering needs to be for three million shares. Again, this is a basic way to think about it, and many other factors are going to alter that equation considerably.

THE PROSPECTUS

The primary document of disclosure distributed to potential investors and included in the registration documentation is known as the prospectus. The SEC describes in detail what is required of the prospectus on the S-1, SB-1, or SB-2 forms.

These directions are specific, and it is quite obvious, even to a beginner, what needs to be included in the prospectus. Equally as important as having a complete prospectus is having a readable one. The SEC has passed a "plain English" rule, meaning that a prospectus must be written so that a layman can understand it. This gives amateur investors a better chance at making an informed decision.

The prospectus is essentially disclosure, and the SEC review process can be a long one. Chances are good that the SEC will require you to make various revisions on your prospectus to present a more accurate picture of your company to the public.

YOUR COMMENT PERIOD

This period of revision is known as the SEC comment period. If this period goes on for too long, you might miss your IPO window. In order to ensure that it does not, back up every assertion you make with hard data. Do not try to slip anything past the SEC comment board.

Look at successful prospectuses and conform yours closely to theirs. Your attorney, accountant, or investment broker can obtain an assortment of prospectuses for you to review.

Once the prospectus is submitted, it can take as long as a week before a decision is reached to review it, and another 30 days before the comment period begins. Once the SEC is satisfied that their comments have been addressed, you can request a date and time for the issue to become effective.

This request is known as the request for acceleration, during which time the approved preliminary prospectus is distributed among the group of potential investors.

SOFT INFORMATION

Opinions, predictions, and educated guesses are known as "soft" information. The SEC calls these "forward-looking statements" and will not challenge them unless they are plainly fraudulent. Careful presentation of soft information can help create an optimistic atmosphere around your IPO, which is what you want. Make sure you discuss all of this with your lawyer before proceeding publicly.

ROAD-SHOW PRESENTATIONS

The road show is a crucial part of garnering interest in the final days before going public. It consists of a nationwide whirlwind tour, with presentations in every major city in the country. If all goes well, you will drive up the price of your securities.

The idea behind the road show is to put you and your team in front of audiences of potential investors. The success of your road show can make or break your IPO, so be prepared for it. Usually this is the management's only venue for proving itself to investors. Team members will need all of their wits about them, as questioning during the road show can be intense and antagonistic. That said, it is important to maintain an air of confidence. If you show any sign of losing confidence, the investors will sense it immediately, and the trip could be a disaster.

Your team's knowledge of their industry and issues of credibility should never be in doubt. Encourage them to keep themselves in peak condition and maintain their decorum throughout.

The two major parts of the road show include:

1. **Presentation**—Rehearsal is critical before taking any presentation on the road. The presentation not only needs to inform and encourage the potential investor, but also to hold their interest as well. Appropriate humor is welcomed.

2. **Q and A**—During this improvised section of your performance, your team is likely to get some pretty nasty questions. Stay positive throughout. Spend plenty of time preparing for questions about your business plan, accounting practices, competition, and any other topics that might be of interest.

Be prepared to address negative issues directly; avoiding topics sends up red flags. What might be a minor issue can grow overnight into a monster if not addressed properly. Practice role-playing scenarios so that you are comfortable fielding these types of queries.

Sometimes investors will try to pressure you into releasing information that is not included in your prospectus. Do not give in to this kind of pressure. Not only could it spoil the whole deal, it could also land you in serious legal trouble.

The road show will be more physically and emotionally

demanding than probably any business experience you have had thus far. But remember, make it through the chaos could be very rewarding.

FINAL PRICING AND CLOSING

This is the end of the road for your IPO. From here on, it is pretty much out of your hands. Your underwriter and the markets will decide the final price of the stock shares. The share price will not be finalized until the offering date, and the same goes for the number of shares offered. The offering date is when your stock first begins being publicly traded; it is the effective date of the IPO.

The IPO closes three business days after the offering date. A small amount of paperwork is needed to finalize the IPO before the bank checks reflecting the IPOs proceeds are disbursed. A well-deserved celebration usually follows.

GARNERING INTEREST

Once your IPO makes it to the stock exchange floor, you need to be absolutely positive that it is going to sell. Here are some ways to maximize your IPO's selling potential:

- Time your IPO when the market is friendly.

- Make sure you are dealing with a top-notch, high-profile investment bank when you go public.

- Have a product or service that sets your business apart, and make sure everyone knows about it.

- Advertise your management team as much as your product, making sure they have the skills and experience to back up all the great things you tell everyone about them.

- Your sales pitch needs to be first-rate, completely professional, and perfectly polished. Make sure that potential investors know who your market is and how you plan to reach it.

YOUR QUIET PERIOD

Once you hire an investment banker, you enter into what is commonly referred to as the "quiet period." This period, mandated by the SEC, lasts until 25 days after the IPO is made.

The quiet period restricts you and your employees from speaking publicly about the IPO to anyone, including your family, unless the information released is in the prospectus. This restriction covers press releases, speeches, and advertising. If you are not sure if you should say it, then remain quiet.

POST-IPO ACTIVITY

Now that your company is public, it should have the cash it needs to grow. There are still certain things to consider:

- Stay involved with your securities.

- Counteract slipping stock prices immediately.

- Maintain investor relations.

- Keep growth steady.

- Enlist analysts to help.

Not staying in the game after the IPO can cause the value of your securities to start slipping, maybe even causing a panic-driven sell-off by investors. Remember, trends in the public market are strong, and once you get caught in a whirlpool, it is difficult to recover.

REWARDS AND CONSEQUENCES

When handled and timed correctly, IPOs can enrich both the entrepreneur and the business. Take Simula, Inc., a manufacturer of airplane components. Simula, valued at $11.9 million, raised $5 million from their IPO. Today, the same company is valued at over $150 million, with common stock trading at around $25 per share. This common stock, because of its steady increase in value, has been used as currency by the company for two acquisitions, further contributing to its growth.

On the other side of the coin is the software company Young Minds, Inc. Counting on the $13.2 million the IPO was expected to raise turned out to be a mistake of epic proportions. The deal fell through, the IPO never happened, and Young Minds was out of money for several months after that.

Young Minds was forced to lay off a third of its workforce, and the partners resorted to taking out second mortgages on their homes in order to provide capital and avoid filing for bankruptcy. An IPO that was supposed to save the business ended up pushing it deeper into the hole.

Unfortunately, this is not an uncommon story. Hundreds of companies every year, pressured by investment banks looking to cash in on a roaring IPO market, suffer the same humiliating fate. As an entrepreneur, knowing the consequences of going public too soon can save a lot of stress and heartache. The great rewards that come from a successful IPO only come with patience, timing, and luck.

UP-TO-DATE INFORMATION

Your legal and financial team will inform you on market conditions and current SEC requirements. In addition, they will advise you on the potential for an IPO. More up-to-date information on IPOs can be found at IPO Financial at **www.ipofinancial.com**.

14

DIRECT PUBLIC OFFERINGS

Businesses are always looking for new ways to raise money. In recent years, a creative new form of stock offering has gained momentum: direct public offering (DPO). A DPO combines the features of "going public" with those of obtaining venture capital.

Regulated and registered in the same way as any other public securities offering, a DPO seeks to raise capital by selling shares of the business's ownership directly to the public. Unlike an IPO, there is no need for a trading market for a DPO to succeed. Stock is issued primarily to those in the business's circle, namely friends, family, customers, suppliers, associates, and colleagues.

Companies conducting a DPO issue and sell their own stock, primarily by way of the Internet. There is no underwriter involved; the company does all of its own structuring, filing, underwriting, and selling. Companies that offer DPOs are usually in the consumer products industry. Food suppliers, restaurants, mail-order companies, and microbreweries are a few examples.

THE FUNCTION OF THE DPO

DPOs can fill an important gap for small business. This "capital chasm," as it is commonly known, exists for many companies that are seeking between $200,000 and $5 million. Funding under $200,000 is typically covered by a loan or acquaintance angel (someone you already know). Amounts over $5 million are usually raised through venture capital or an IPO.

Although complex, the DPO becomes an important option to consider for entrepreneurs who are not comfortable with an angel or for those who simply cannot find a compatible angel investor. DPOs should be strongly considered by companies who have a solid customer base, but want to increase their growth potential. These companies are too small to attract venture capitalists or investment bankers, but they have grown too much to rely on family and friends or SBA microloans.

DIFFERENT WAYS TO PROCEED

Depending on the needs of your company, DPOs may be filed in different ways. Each strategy involves both federal and state laws, so check thoroughly and consult your legal and financial advisers to choose the DPO best for your business.

State and federal exemption laws can govern the way a DPO is conducted, or it can work the same way as an IPO, using a full registration process with the SEC. Individual businesses must consider several factors:

- How much money needs to be raised.

- Whether the business wants its stock traded on the market.

- If the company is able to provide audited financial statements.

- How many investors will be involved.

- If the business wants to solicit or advertise for the DPO.

Registering in Full with the SEC

In order to have the opportunity to have your stock traded publicly through NASDAQ, you must complete a full registration with the SEC. This process involves the same amount of paperwork as an IPO but without the assistance of a brokerage firm or team of investment bankers.

Filing Through Regulation A

If you want to raise no less than $1 million, but no more than $5 million, Regulation A is the best DPO option. It will exempt your business from federal registration under Regulation A of the Securities Act of 1933.

Another benefit of Regulation A is that the federal government does not require audited financial statements of your business. Keep in mind, however, that this is still required in certain states, under state law.

Small Company Offering Registration

Also known as SCOR, this method of filing is limited to those who wish to raise less than $1 million in a DPO. The form, known as form U-7, is complicated and a difficult undertaking in and of itself.

SCOR registration is available in 46 states, as well as in the District of Columbia. Alabama, Delaware, Hawaii, and

Nebraska do not accept the SCOR registration form.

OTHER EXEMPTIONS

There are ways to avoid filings of any kind. At the federal level, this exemption is known as Regulation D. At the state level, the deal must be structured around that particular state's exemption laws.

THE BENEFITS OF A DPO

The benefits of issuing a DPO over other financing include:

1. Equity raised through the sale of stock does not have to be repaid.

2. You retain a greater share of ownership than when dealing with venture capitalists or public stock offerings.

3. It costs less to finance a DPO. DPOs can usually be financed for well under $100,000 as opposed to an IPO that can cost into the millions.

4. You can learn about investment banking before jumping into the deep end of the lake.

5. Your public offering can benefit current customers, suppliers, and employees who already have a vested interest in your success.

6. You can test market your ability to raise equity via your stock offering by advertising a potential stock sale.

7. Internet-offered DPOs give you the ability to reach a niche market of potential investors with a specific affinity

for your products or services. More and more people spend personal time seeking investment opportunities online.

8. You can market your DPO while you are marketing your company and products. Your marketing can be directed to potential customers who like the idea of being a part of something.

9. You become a publicly held company, elevating your status.

10. You increase your ability to obtain other types of financing.

THE TROUBLE WITH A DPO

Although DPOs seem like the way to go for companies that can't afford a stellar PR firm, a big investment bank affiliation, a securities lawyer, and a stockbroker, is it possible for a business management team to play all these roles themselves? Many professionals think not.

Also, many small, early-stage businesses simply do not run a tight enough ship to stand up under public scrutiny. Running a business and justifying the way you run your business to the public are two entirely different things.

Another problem with DPOs is the time they take from the founder. Running a business is difficult enough, but trying to run one while handling a public offering scenario can be a Herculean task. Founders should seriously consider whether or not they have the stamina to handle these things simultaneously.

Although managing a DPO can seem to some like managing any other kind of project, other factors need to be considered. For instance, there is little to no chance that a founder would sell his or her stocks to investors while undertaking a DPO. This means that the entrepreneur does not really stand to gain financially from the DPO, as they would in an IPO.

Moreover, the stock has no value as currency because there is no trading market. In other words, acquiring companies by giving them stock instead of cash is an impossibility.

Finally, if your company has early-stage investors who are looking for an exit strategy, a DPO does not offer that option. Misinterpreting a DPO as a general substitute for an IPO will get you into trouble with current investors, who may be looking to cash out on the deal.

Other negatives you might encounter with a DPO include:

- Many people are unfamiliar with a DPO, requiring you to spend an inordinate amount of time explaining the process.

- It is a time-intensive do-it-yourself process.

- Investment specialists note a high failure rate for this type of offering.

- It is more difficult to find legal and financial experts with DPO experience.

SELLING YOUR DPO

After your SEC and state filings have been completed and approved, it is up to you and your team to market and sell your stock. Remember, no stock exchange is involved so you will not be listed for investors to find. To reach your established goals, your management team, your employees, and even your family will become active and assertive salespeople.

Creative marketing and selling techniques make the difference when raising cash via a DPO. If you are uncomfortable pitching yourself and your company, then a DPO may not be right for you.

Here are a few of the creative marketing techniques that entrepreneurs have used to sell stock:

1. A coffee roaster placed announcements in his coffee shop, dropped notes into bags of ground coffee, sent notices to vendors, and purchased ads talking about his stock offering.

2. A homeopathic pharmacy targeted people interested in alternative medicine via direct mail campaigns. His direct mail list came from vitamin catalog buyers and natural health magazine subscribers.

3. The biologist owners of a pharmaceutical startup hosted cocktail parties and open houses to discuss their offering with industry peers and local investors.

Creativity in promoting your stock offering increases your potential for raising cash; however, high-pressure sales tactics can backfire and leave your company with a tainted image.

THE POWER OF THE INTERNET

Small businesses have been pioneers in using the Internet both to garner interest in their companies and to raise capital. The

Internet continues to be a valid resource for marketing and selling your DPO, although that wasn't always the case.

Spring Street Brewing Company was one of the first microbreweries and one of the first small businesses to raise capital through a DPO. In 1995 they raised $1.6 million in capital, without the expense of hiring an underwriter.

The SEC granted Spring Street permission to use the Internet as the primary source for finding investors. This approach, coupled with advertising directly to consumers by printing directly on their product, in this case bottles of beer, generated extraordinary interest in the company, and, as a result, a huge increase in capital.

Because of the publicity surrounding this success story, many more small businesses turned to the DPO as a source of potential funding. The Internet looked to be an inexpensive and effective way to generate capital directly from the public. Many soon learned, though, that it was not as easy as it appeared to be. In fact, Spring Street Brewing eventually closed their doors.

The Internet is a valuable tool for distribution of information. It is not, however, the most effective selling tool. Potential investors have become accustomed to skipping over advertisements in order to get to what they set out to find.

When attempting to raise money via the Internet, it is important to make sure that:

- The Web site is easy to locate so that your target investors can find it.

- The investors that find the site live in the same state as you so that they are eligible to buy the offering.

- The site arouses curiosity within the investor, so much so that they are willing to download your prospectus.

- Once downloaded, your prospectus convinces them that your company is worth an investment.

- The information provided to the investor about the business via the prospectus does not get used against the entrepreneur.

- The investor will follow through and buy shares in the company.

- The company takes measures so that if the investor does not send a check, they can be convinced to do so.

- Enough investors take advantage of the offering so that the deal can be closed successfully.

- The deal is closed in a reasonable period of time.

Web DPO Sales

Releasing, promoting, and selling your DPO via the Internet takes more effort than just posting a banner ad on your existing Web site. With the growing interest in DPOs, the number of online consultants has also grown. When hiring any sort of consultant, take time to research, check references, and ask questions. Avoid firms that promise "guaranteed results." Your CPA or business development consultant should be able to help you choose a DPO adviser.

Here are a few questions to ask before enlisting outside help:

1. How many years has the consultant been in business?

2. May I speak with previous customers?

3. What personal education and experience do the principals have?

4. What experience does the consultant have in your specific industry?

5. What is the consultant's success ratio?

6. What are the basic fees? additional ongoing fees?

Do not rely on the Internet to make the DPO for you. Recognize it for what it is—a very effective marketing tool, but one of many marketing tools available to your company. Be creative, and do not let the Internet box you in to thinking that it is the only way to a successful DPO. There are always new ways to reach potential investors, and one of your jobs as an entrepreneur is to find those ways.

DPO ADVICE

As it turns out, DPOs can be as work as an IPO, but with less money involved. The decision to make a DPO can seriously affect the future of your business, and it should be handled as carefully as any other major business move is handled.

Certain industries tend to be better suited to DPOs. These include businesses whose clients are major businesses themselves or whose customer base is broad but intimate enough to substantiate putting their money forth.

The most successful industries seem to be:

- Beer and wine

- Food and beverage

- Environmental agencies

- Mail-order retailers

- Clothing retailers

- Restaurants that know their clientele very well

THE DPO PROJECT MANAGER

The CEO or founder of the business is not always the best person to head up the DPO. They are usually too busy dealing with the day-to-day operations of the business to give it their full attention.

Assigning the task to a specific, capable person already on the payroll is common, as is hiring someone new specifically for the task or outsourcing the job to a firm that specializes in handling DPOs for small companies. Whoever takes on the job, it should be the only thing they are expected to handle. They are technically taking on a job normally done by four or five people during a standard IPO filing.

If you are interested in using a DPO to raise money for your company, look into the following:

- SEC laws and regulations concerning DPOs in your state.

- Ask businesses in your industry that have issued a DPO about their experiences.

- Be selective about who you choose to become a partner in your business, making sure they have an active interest in the company itself, not just in making money from it.

- Research the Internet DPO market carefully, making sure that it is legitimate.

- When using a firm that specializes in Internet DPOs, get referrals to ensure that the company you are dealing with is on the level.

Plan ahead. Do all of the research and put everything in place far ahead of the actual date of the offering.

CHAPTER

15

STRATEGIC ALLIANCES

Having allies is as important in business as it is in life. If an entrepreneur can realize the opportunity for an alliance, then they have realized an opportunity to raise capital and to promote the business.

Strategic alliances are mutually beneficial arrangements between two or more businesses. For instance, if you use a specific product frequently in your business, your supplier may offer discounts or incentives in exchange for promotion of the product or for a promise that you will use that product exclusively.

Alternatively, if your Web site draws a certain demographic, companies catering to that same demographic may pay you to appear on your site or help you finance projects they believe will help their sales.

Alliances work the other way too. If you supply a company with a certain product, you may want to offer discounts or incentives to carry your products exclusively or to promote your products by, say, placing your logo on their uniforms.

Likewise, seeking Web sites that cater to your customers is also a good idea. Ideally, you should be able to strike an arrangement to get your product promoted without having to surrender cash.

Strategic alliances can often lead to long-standing relationships with other companies, helping both companies grow simultaneously. These companies may also be able to help you generate leads for future rounds of investor financing. Allying yourself with other small businesses and networking often go hand in hand.

As usual, some caution should be exercised. Carefully evaluate the business with which you are about to enter into a strategic alliance. If anything causes you to hesitate, it would, of course, be best not to associate with their business. Do not be afraid to terminate alliances, either, if you feel like the business you've allied with has started to decline.

MERGERS

A merger is when one company purchases and absorbs another. Mergers are frequently used as an exit strategy for founders and investors. Clearly, a great deal of money stands to be made through the sale of a business.

Mergers are, in fact, a more popular exit strategy than IPOs. Entrepreneurs cash out all the time by having their business acquired by a larger corporation. It is the shareholders of the company who decide whether or not the merger is to be made. This is decided by vote, and, depending on the state, either a simple majority or two-thirds majority will carry the decision forward. When the vote is not unanimous, and many of the shareholders disagree with the decision to sell the company (though, obviously, not enough to constitute a majority), the merger is then known as a "forced" merger. The dissenting shareholders do have certain rights, however, and can take the business to court if they believe they are have been treated unfairly.

Not to be confused with a merger, a consolidation is when a large corporation is created and each business involved is merged into the new corporation. This is the corporate version of the cliché that there is safety in numbers.

The four main types of mergers are:

1. The triangular merger.

2. The forward merger.

3. The reverse merger.

4. The reverse triangular merger.

The Triangular Merger

This type of merger occurs when a large corporation wishes to combine one of its subsidiaries with a smaller independent company. Though the two smaller ventures are the ones ultimately being combined, the parent company is the one who buys out the independent, not the subsidiary. The name comes from the triangular shape that is formed when you consider the parent company, the subsidiary, and the acquired company.

The Forward Merger

When one company acquires another, and the charter, or certificate of incorporation, of the acquiring company survives, it is known as a forward merger.

The Reverse Merger

When one company acquires another, but the acquired company's certificate of incorporation (charter) does not survive, it is known as a reverse merger.

The Reverse Triangular Merger

Large companies will often create subsidiaries specifically for the purpose of a merger. Once the subsidiary is in place, a reverse merger occurs between the subsidiary and the acquired company. The acquired company then becomes a subsidiary of the parent corporation. This is perhaps the most common form of merger.

TAXABLE AND TAX-POSTPONED MERGERS

If a company is purchased outright with cash, then the income each shareholder receives is obviously taxable. But, if the shareholders are willing to take stock in the acquiring company in lieu of cash, then paying the taxes on the sale can be postponed until the shareholder decides to cash out.

There is usually a minimum period of time that the shareholders must wait before cashing in their stocks. If the acquired company is public, however, this is sometimes a non-issue, and the shareholders can sell or diversify after closing, pending SEC regulations and controls.

COMMON MERGER PROCEDURES

As previously stated, no deal should be made without consulting professionals and without having a team of experts by your side to help you through the deal. A merger is no different, and is, in fact, one of the more complicated types of agreements.

Mergers are not uniform procedures. The following is simply a general guideline to help entrepreneurs understand the basics of merging their company with another, possibly cashing out in the process.

Positioning the Company

Maintaining both strategic alliances and partnerships are a good way of finding parties that may be interested in a merger. If you expect a good valuation of your company, then the acquiring company needs to be genuinely interested.

Waiting for the right time to position your company is important for a merger as well. Keep track of valuations of companies in your industry that are similar to your company. If you notice these valuations begin to rise, it might be a good time to think about merging.

Assembling the Team and Garnering Support

The merger will not go anywhere if the board of directors do not support the idea 100 percent. Put together a team of your most trusted staff, a good merger attorney, an accountant who specializes in acquisitions, and an investment banker or two, and make your presentation to the board.

Once the board is behind the goal, preparations need to be made. It is again time to update the business plan to make it look appealing to an acquiring company. Make a thorough list of prospects, and conduct an audit and valuation of the business.

Draft a very clear nondisclosure agreement for everyone involved to sign. If word gets out that the owner is planning to sell the company before the arrangements are completed, the result could be a panic that sends your company into a downward spiral.

Contacting Prospective Buyers

If you think a business would be interested in acquiring your company, contact its CEO. Arrange a meeting and have them sign the nondisclosure agreement. After the meeting they may make a bid, usually one that is far too low. Begin negotiations.

Having two or three bidders is ideal, as this can drive up the price for your company as each prospect attempts to outbid the other. Although it seems as if you were lucky to receive an offer at all, it is usually best to wait and negotiate before accepting a bid.

More than two or three bidders, however, can be overwhelming. Narrow the competition once it becomes clear which bidders are the most serious about acquiring your company.

Moving to Close

When you have a good idea who you want to sell to, begin negotiating the final price. The buyer will, of course, begin low. They will also want to know how you arrived at your asking price, so know the justifications of your valuation very well. Have comparables close at hand to show to the prospect, as evidence that you are asking a fair price.

Letter of Intent

This letter of intent (LOI) is an outline of the deal, created with the buyer. It should contain:

1. Names of those involved and exactly what is being acquired by whom.

2. What kind of consideration this is, along with price and any earn-outs (parts of the price contingent upon the achievement of future business goals).

3. Legalities and transaction form.

4. Closing conditions, a list of the things still to be negotiated before the deal can close.

5. Confidentiality statement, making your nondisclosure agreement valid and forbidding public disclosure of the deal until both parties agree to it.

6. The LOI expiration date (when the LOI terminates, effectively placing a deadline on when negotiations must be completed by, usually within 30 to 90 days).

Due Diligence Period

The prospective buyer will commence with due diligence the same way a venture capitalist or an angel might, carefully considering the risk of the acquisition versus the possible return on what is, in their eyes, an investment.

Definitive Agreement, Voting, and Closing

A definitive agreement is signed once the terms of the deal are finalized. If either company is public, an announcement must

be made at this point. The shareholders of both companies will
then vote.

If the shareholders vote in favor of the merger, then the deal is
officially closed. A new board of directors takes over, and the
acquiring company assumes control of business operations.

WHEN TO DISCLOSE THE DEAL

It is crucial not to let your employees, lenders, suppliers, or
customers discover too soon that you intend to sell the business.
This is where the nondisclosure agreement comes in. Keep track
of who has been told what, and make sure that all parties have
signed a nondisclosure agreement.

When the deal is finalized, and it comes time to tell everyone
else, be prepared for a barrage of panicked questions. Your
employees will certainly want to know if their jobs are secure as
well as if their compensation packages will change.

Have the buyer begin working with your company to outline
exactly what changes, if any, they intend to make within the
acquired company. Your employees should be able to meet with
their new supervisors in order to ask questions.

Customers also need to be handled gently, and the buyer needs
to assume the responsibility of making sure they know that their
service or product will continue to be provided, regardless of
the change of ownership.

For everyone else, a simple press release is an adequate way to
let people know that the business has been acquired.

LEVERAGE

There are generally two types of leverage: financial leverage and operating leverage. Financial leverage is the debt-to-equity ratio of your business. Operating leverage is the ratio of fixed to variable costs. The higher your leverage, the more of a risk your business is considered by lenders.

Leverage means different things to different types of investors and bankers. The term is quite vague, and the methods for determining leverage are diverse. Make sure you know how your bank determines your leverage, so you can point out anything that might be misinterpreted as negative.

For instance, if you have what are known as friendly debts, meaning debts that are owed to people involved with your company or who have a personal stake in you, these debts should not be factored when determining leverage.

Because leverage is one way a bank determines how risky your business is, it is important to keep it low. One of the goals of your business should be to lower leverage from year to year.

Financial Leverage

Financial leverage is calculated by comparing how much debt the business has versus how much equity. Banks typically look for at least a 3:1 leverage rate before approving a loan.

This means that for every three dollars of money that the bank gives the business in the form of a loan, the founder is expected to contribute a dollar of his or her own money. Of course, the more equity there is, the lower the rates of return on that equity.

Having high leverage can make it very difficult to get a bank loan. This is because when a company has high leverage, it is volatile. If sales happen to increase when a company is highly leveraged, then high returns can be expected. But if sales drop by an equal amount, then the equity of the business can be wiped out quickly.

As the business grows, its financial leverage has a tendency to change. If the business is successful, it will hopefully lower, making it easier for the company to acquire debt financing in the future.

Operating Leverage

Operating leverage is the ratio between the fixed costs and the variable costs of your business. The higher the ratio, the higher your leverage, and therefore the higher the risk level of your venture.

Fixed costs are costs that do not change for your business over a specific period of time, regardless of how the business is doing in terms of sales and output. Rent, lease, and loan payments are examples of fixed costs.

Variable costs, on the other hand, do change according to the sales figures. How much material to buy, how much advertising to do, and how much travel needs to be done are examples of variable costs.

Payroll may or may not be a variable cost, depending on the size and nature of the business. Most small businesses do not employ too many people, and those people tend to remain, so payroll is usually treated as a fixed cost.

If the business tends toward a low percentage of fixed costs and higher variable costs, then it does not require as much money for your business to break even. This is seen as good by the banks because it is considered less risky.

If the business tends to have a high percentage of fixed costs, then the volume of business that must be done is much greater in order to break even. This is seen as risky, and banks may demand a change in the cost structure before doing business.

It is important that your legal counsel be familiar with the rules and regulations governing business in your particular state as well as the states that affect your business.

16 LEGAL CONSIDERATIONS

Many laws regulate how and when a small business can raise capital. Some of these rules are governed by the Small Business Administration, while others (mostly those having to do with stocks and public offerings) are governed by the Securities and Exchange Commission.

Still other laws vary from state to state, so it is important that your legal counsel be familiar with the rules and regulations governing business in your particular state as well as the states that affect your business.

The following outlines are distillations of the general concepts surrounding the laws. They should not be considered a substitute for legal counsel or as documentation of the laws themselves.

ACCREDITED INVESTORS

Accredited investors and investment firms are those firms, as defined by law, that are wealthy enough to handle the risks of investing in private equity markets. The reason for the accreditation process is to prevent people from taking risks their finances cannot absorb when dealing in illiquid equity.

The general guidelines for an accredited investor are as follows:

1. They must make at least $200,000 a year, and must have been at that rate of income for the past two years, and anticipate that rate of income for the coming year. If dealing with a combined income (a spouse), the required income level is $300,000.

2. Their minimum net worth must be at least $1 million. This applies for combined net worth as well.

BLUE-SKY STATUTES

State regulations were passed (the earliest in 1911) to try to protect investors from fraudulent securities offerings. These were known as blue-sky statutes, and they were constantly modified and updated.

Most blue-sky statutes no longer apply when dealing with private equity offerings (due to the National Securities Market Improvement Act of 1996), but it would be wise to see what statutes still exist in your state.

CONFLICTS OF INTEREST

This is mostly a tax issue having to do with insider dealings in the business. For instance, if an employee is offered a substantial discount on a substantial purchase, this discount can be considered taxable income.

Another example would be if the business rented its offices from the founder. A founder can avoid this conflict by using the sell-

and-release technique, which also gives the business an infusion of cash if the founder wants to invest in it.

THE EQUAL CREDIT OPPORTUNITY ACT

This act prevents lenders from denying you a loan or line of credit based on your race, religion, creed, or sex. If you are rejected, you are permitted under this act to find out why. The lender is obligated, if you are a small business, to retain your records for a full year in case you believe you have been treated unfairly and wish to file suit.

LEGALITIES CONCERNING INVESTMENTS FROM FAMILY AND FRIENDS

When borrowing money from family and friends, the founder assumes certain legal responsibilities in order to avoid getting sued in the future. These include:

- Full disclosure to the investor.

- Only soliciting as much as the non-accredited investor can afford to lose.

- Valuing the company fairly.

- Frequent reporting to investors.

- Complete a valid buy-sell agreement.

IPO REGULATIONS

The number of laws and regulations regarding IPOs are numerous. These include:

- Filing periodic reports with the SEC.

- Filing flash reports with the SEC when any major event occurs.

- Full disclosure reports to the SEC each year, including information about management's compensation.

- Ensuring public investors receive information at the same time as institutional investors and analysts.

- Key team members can trade only during specific windows of time as part of the SEC's anti-insider trading laws.

PRIVATE PLACEMENT MEMORANDUM

A legal document that must be prepared before making a private equity offering, the private placement memorandum (PPM) exists so that the founder can avoid liability for misstatements and omissions that may occur when filling out the paperwork for the offering.

A PPM is not always necessary when the offering is small enough or when certain exemptions apply. Consulting a lawyer on whether or not a PPM is appropriate is a must, as preparation of any document of this magnitude can consume time, resources, and money.

ANGEL SOLICITATION

The SEC forbids "general advertising or general solicitation" of angel investors. What this statement means is relatively unclear, so consult with a lawyer before promoting the fact that your business is seeking funding.

SECURITIES REGULATIONS

Rule 504 of SEC Regulation D

Offerings raising less than $1 million in a 12-month period do not have to be registered on the federal level.

The entrepreneur can either:

1. Use the Model Short Form, meaning that they make the offering only to accredited investors in states where the Model Accredited Investor Exemption (MAIE) or other state exemption has been put into effect.

2. If offering to the general public or accredited investors residing in states where the MAIE has not been passed, register with each state that the offering is made within individually. Research each state's laws to know which forms must be filed.

SEC Rule 1001

Offerings of less than $5 million are exempt from registration when made only to "qualified purchasers," which is different from an accredited investor. The only state currently offering this is California. A qualified purchaser is an individual as defined by Paragraph (N), Section 25102 of the California Corporation Code.

The Model Accredited Investor Exemption

Based on the theory that accredited investors are able to perform their own due diligence process and can clearly ascertain the risks of investing in private securities, the MAIE exempts companies making offerings of $1 million or less from registering with the state.

These are a but a handful of the SEC's multitude of regulations, which change constantly and vary from state to state. Stay updated and consult with your lawyer before making any sort of equity offering.

CHAPTER

17

THE PITCH

S earching and securing startup or improvement capital requires confidence, assertiveness, and diligence. This chapter will help prepare you for "pitching" your ideas to potential outside investors and lenders.

FIRST IMPRESSIONS ARE CRITICAL

If you want to "wow" them, you must be prepared physically, mentally, and emotionally. Unless you are a seasoned salesperson, the process of presenting and closing a deal may make your palms sweat, your lips go dry, and your voice crack. Remember: Investors invest in people, not products or ideas. You must sell yourself first.

Looking Good—Physical Preparedness

The axiom "dress for success" certainly applies when you are seeking money. Dressing well sends a message and makes you feel confident. Unless you are a fashion designer showing off your own designs, dressing business conservative is best. This is true even in today's more casual business setting.

Dressing conservatively isn't a matter of "business boring" but of respect. Avoid distractions, including cleavage. Your goal is to have people pay attention to you as a person and to what you say.

Men

For men, a conservative black, gray, medium to dark blue or brown suit with a white or pale blue dress shirt and a coordinating tie. If your suit is more than a few years old, invest in a new one. Check out the men's department at a local department store for current fashions. Specialty men's stores are great resources for helping you look the part of a confident businessman.

Here are some additional dress-for-success tips for men:

- Shoes should be black or dark brown (brown shoes work with some blue suits and all brown suits).

- Socks should match the pants.

- Belts should match the shoes.

- Send your suit (pants and coat) to the cleaners so that when you're ready for the big meeting, all you have to do is dress.

- Polish and shine your shoes and your leather briefcase.

- Use aftershave and cologne sparingly.

- If you want to feel a bit more polished, invest in a manicure and facial. (Avoid facials right before meetings as they can leave your skin red.)

- Practice wearing your selected outfit(s). Can you easily reach, bend, or sit? Does it wrinkle easily? Do you have to loosen your belt? Comfort is important in stressful situations.

Women

Conservative dressing for women usually means a dress or skirt. However, if you are a woman who feels more comfortable in pants, look for a matching jacket and pant set in natural (linen, cotton, wool) fabric. A good-fitting suit is as important to a woman as it is to a man, so have yours tailored if necessary. Women have a broader range of colors that are considered conservative—black, grey, dark green, brown, taupe, mauve. You may add a small accent color in a scarf or pin.

Here are some additional dress-for-success tips for women:

- No sleeveless dresses (unless covered by a jacket), no cleavage, no ankles on display (if you are wearing slacks), no visible tattoos or belly rings. Eliminate distractions.

- Shoes should be comfortable and stylish; leave the dating/dancing shoes at home.

- Women's shoes can be notoriously uncomfortable and soles can be slick. Wear them in advance to "break them in."

- Stockings are a must. Select a natural color; no deep bronze or black. Try them on the day before to check for snags, runs, and fit.

- Keep scarves, bows, ties, and belts under control. Do not wear anything that you will have to fuss with to keep looking right.

- Wear nice jewelry but nothing that clangs, bangs, or distracts.

- Wear fragrance sparingly.

- Makeup should emphasize your natural beauty, no glittery eye shadow or bright red lipstick. Make certain your hair and nails look professional.

- Invest in a great briefcase. Do not carry a handbag if you carry a briefcase.

- Try a dress rehearsal. Look for skirts that hike up, items that wrinkle too easily, waistbands that bind, and undergarments that create bulges.

Exceptions to the Rules

Business can be conducted virtually anywhere—on the golf course, during a game of handball, on a commuter train, or at a convention. Imagine walking on a putting green in high heels! If the situation is outside of the usual business environment, feel free to break the dress-conservative rules. The key is appropriateness.

If in doubt, ask about appropriate attire. Ask the party planner, executive's assistant, or an intermediary about what to wear. Check the weather report so you can bring an umbrella, wear a lighter-weight blouse, or exchange the wool suit for a linen one.

Some industries by nature are more colorful and casual. Your style of dress may reflect what you do for a living. During your dress rehearsal, stand in front of a full-length mirror and look at yourself from every angle. Would you trust this person with your money?

HIGH ANXIETY

Often the body signals that it is in a state of anxiety. If nervousness causes you to sweat excessively, jumbles your speech, or makes you shake, here are some things you can do to tame the physical symptoms:

- Sweaty palms are a common sign of nervous tension. Apply invisible antiperspirant with the active ingredient aluminum chlorohydrate to your palms before leaving home.

- Breathe deeply multiple times before leaving the car, elevator, or stairway. The increased oxygen calms and clears your head.

- Don't overcompensate for nerves or you will appear too stiff or aloof. You are human and so are the people you are meeting — they will overlook a bit of jitters.

- Eat lightly before hand. Avoid coffee, dairy products, or anything that creates gas.

- Speak slowly. Nervousness can make you speed up and overlook important points.

- Think positively. Give yourself a confidence-boosting pep talk.

- Arrive early to minimize the last-minute panic. Take the extra minutes to walk around a bit to stretch, relax, and use the restroom. Do not arrive more than five to seven minutes early, as this can create a stressful situation for your audience.

- Keep your emotions to yourself. Do not confess that you are nervous, as this shifts the focus of your presentation from what you are saying to how you are saying it. Empathy can backfire when the listener becomes distracted from your message.

GETTING YOUR BRAIN READY— MENTAL PREPAREDNESS

Yes, you will be nervous, but there are some pre-presentation activities you can do to help you prepare mentally. Mental preparedness is a way of training your mind to keep your fears, anxieties, and emotions from tripping you during presentations.

Don't Worry

As with most things in life, 90 percent of what we worry about never happens. Use various exercises such as journaling, worst-case-scenario exploration, or even setting aside worry time. Try the ACT formula (as detailed in *Rapid Relief from Emotional Distress* by Gary Emery, Ph.D. and James Campbell, M.D.).

Use Fear

Fear also can be a stimulus for top performance. Think of your fear as untapped energy. Imagine re-channeling that energy through your body to increase your confidence, steady your nerves, and feel powerful!

YOUR IDEAS (AND SOUL) ON DISPLAY—EMOTIONAL PREPAREDNESS

You have spent months (and perhaps even years) working on your new business idea. No doubt, you are proud of your idea and, frankly and understandably, you are biased about its growth potential. Emotional preparedness will help with the possibility and probability of rejection. Emotional issues arise from positive outcomes too, so prepare for those as well.

KNOW THE TRUTH

There are some business truths you should know. Understanding how things work can help you deal with frustrations, self-doubts, and lagging confidence.

1. Sometimes you will not click. You have found the right investor for your new invention, but she is not interested. Investors rely on personal interest, business savvy, gut instincts, a sense of adventure, and luck when they choose a project. Sometimes there is not a solid reason that an investor says no.

2. Life can get in the way. You are in the last stages of launching a new hamburger stand, when Mad Cow disease hits your community. Fear keeps people from buying beef temporarily. Unfortunate events have made this a bad time to invest in meat-based companies. Although the event that trips you may not be headline worthy, situations can derail your ability to acquire outside funding.

3. Timing is everything. Your plan was well-received. You can see the investors' interest. However, there is no

money for you. Investment groups may allocate funds to different types of ventures to reduce risks. Your idea is good, but the entrepreneur before you got the last allocation.

4. No is not the end. As with the timing example above, no may only mean "not right now." Ask about the reasons for the negative response. This is a learning opportunity and a chance to make changes before your next presentation.

5. Yes can mean no. In your eagerness to hear the "yes," do not overlook negative conditions or the "Yes, but…" answer. Know what you are willing to give or change to receive the funds you need.

DEALING WITH NO

Do not let "no" derail you emotionally. Because you've worked so hard and invested so much of yourself, you are especially susceptible to disappointment and even depression. Allow yourself a couple of days to feel disappointed, and then clear your head for the next steps.

After being turned down for a loan or investor dollars, make a list of what you have personally learned from the experience. The good news is that people do not typically get together to talk about your poor presentation, so you can turn this into a "practice" experience without embarrassment.

PASSION SPEAKS

One of the best ways to eliminate presentation fears is to speak with passion. The passion within you feels natural and reduces your stress—and you are more likely to convince others that the passion is well-founded.

REHEARSE, REHEARSE, REHEARSE

The best way to combat nervousness is to prepare in advance for the meeting and presentation. "Stage fright" is normal— even for the people you are meeting.

Preparation is not memorizing your presentation. It is:

- Feeling comfortable speaking with decision-makers.

- Making certain you cover all your critical points.

- Keeping your sentences clear.

- Honing your ability to respond to questions or unforeseen events.

Rehearsal for the big day can be done by doing the following:

- Role-playing with a trusted friend. Encourage them to ask any question that pops into their head. You will learn how to respond quickly and appropriately.

- Full dress rehearsal. This gives you the opportunity to feel comfortable in your clothing and to check for problem issues. It also provides a sensory memory to recall to help you "remember" that you have done this successfully before.

- Videotape yourself. A camcorder and tripod setup can help you see how others will see you. Do not be too hard on yourself. Remember, you are not a professional speaker and no one expects you to be. Concentrate on eliminating the "ums" and "ahs" and learn how to pause, breathe, and continue naturally.

- Note-card training. Practice what you will say using note cards until you can slowly minimize the need.

- Question-and-answer brainstorming. Write down all the different types of questions a lender or investor might ask you and prepare responses. Practice a natural pause to help you collect your thoughts before answering.

READY FOR SUCCESS

The big day is almost here and you will present your idea to a group of local angel investors. You have selected your attire, prepared your notes, and practiced answering questions. Here are a few additional preparation steps to help everything go smoothly:

1. Find out the pronunciation of unusual names. Colleagues and receptionists can be helpful.

2. Confirm the meeting date and time at least one day ahead of your appointment.

3. Map your route and drive it to estimate travel time. Getting lost and arriving late will count against you.

4. Learn the equipment. If you are giving any type of multi-media presentation (PowerPoint, video, slide, overhead projector), make certain you know how to operate and troubleshoot the hardware and software. If you require electricity, a screen, or other accessories, ask about availability.

5. Concentrate on your audience. Even if that is just you and a lender, think about them and not about yourself to reduce the tension. Remember, this is not a hostile encounter; the audience wants this to be a productive meeting for everyone.

6. Incorporate visuals. A 10- to 15-slide PowerPoint presentation can reinforce specific points and keep investors listening.

Searching and securing startup
or improvement capital requires
confidence, assertiveness, and diligence.

CHAPTER

18 **GLOSSARY**

Accredited investor: A private investor deemed wealthy enough to be able to afford losses on risky private offerings.

Angel investor: Someone of high net worth who invests in startup or early-stage companies, often acting as a mentor or adviser as well.

Blue-sky statutes: State laws that govern the sale of securities.

Common stock: Publicly traded stock representing a small fraction of a company's equity.

Consolidation: An umbrella company formed with the specific intention of absorbing several other business entities.

Debt financing: Borrowing money, usually in the form of a loan, and being charged a fee for its use, usually in the form of interest.

Dilution: An investor's percentage of ownership is reduced by additional stock issued during future rounds of financing.

Due diligence: The process by which investors and venture capitalists research a company to make sure it depicts an accurate image of itself in its business plan. This process ultimately decides whether or not the investment is made.

Equity: The ownership of a business or property.

Equity financing: Giving up a portion of the ownership of a business or property in exchange for a cash investment.

Exit strategy: For investors, how and when they will receive the return on their investment. For founders, how and when they will compensate themselves for making the business a success, usually either by selling the business or by selling the stock they have in the business.

Fair market value: The value at which a business would sell if both the buyer and seller were equally willing and informed about the business and industry.

Illiquid securities: Stock that cannot be readily converted into cash.

Initial public offering (IPO): The first sale of stock by a company to the public.

Investment bank: A firm that helps make new companies public by underwriting their offerings.

Issuer: A company that is selling its stock or other securities.

Lease: A contract stating that equipment owned by the lessor (the company that owns the equipment) may be used and possessed by the lessee (the company that needs the equipment) in exchange for regular cash payments.

Letter of intent (LOI): This is signed before a merger to open up the negotiations of terms and conditions. It is a nonbinding document.

Merger: When one company acquires another, or one company is acquired by another, or the two companies are joined.

Nondisclosure agreement: A document signed by two or more negotiating parties, agreeing not to share information about one another with those outside of the negotiations.

Private equity offering: Small stakes in a business sold directly to select individuals or firms, but not to the general public.

Prospectus: The main disclosure document in a public offering, used to sell the offering to investors by giving them a detailed look at the operations of the business.

Receivables financing: A loan borrowed against a company's accounts receivable, usually a short-term, high-interest loan.

Regulation D: An SEC regulation allowing certain private offerings that meet certain conditions exempt from federal registration.

Road show: A tour of major cities in the United States by the management team and underwriters of an IPO just prior to the offering date, designed to garner investment interest in the business.

SEC: The Securities and Exchange Commission. A federal commission regulating the sale and trade of securities in the United States.

Seed capital: The money a small business needs to start work on a prototype (alpha test) of their product in order to prove that it works.

Underwriter: Usually an investment bank that acts as the go-between for the issuer of a security and the public trading market.

Valuation: The process of assigning a fair market value to a business.

Venture capital: Money from venture capital funds given to growing businesses in exchange for substantial portions of equity and control.

CHAPTER

19

RESOURCES

ANGEL INVESTOR RESOURCES

Online Resources

Angel Investor Network at
www.angel-investor-network.com

How To at **www.how-to.com/Operations/
angel-investor.htm**

Inc. article at **www.inc.com/articles/2001/09/23461.html**

Bizology info at **www.bizology.com/finance/angels.html**

Cloudstart at **www.cloudstart.com/site1.php**

Other Resources

*Angel Investing: Matching Startup Funds with Startup
Companies—A Guide for Entrepreneurs, Individual Investors,
and Venture Capitalists* by Mark Van Osnabrugge, Robert
J. Robinson, Mark Van Osnabrugge, Robert J. Robinson.
Publisher: Jossey-Bass (May 2000)

Attracting Capital from Angels: How Their Money—And Their Experience—Can Help You Build a Successful Company by Brian E. Hill, Dee Power. Publisher: Wiley (January 25, 2002)

Every Business Needs an Angel: Getting the Money You Need to Make Your Business Grow by John May, Cal Simons. Publisher: Crown Business; 1st Edition (September 18, 2001)

The Angel Investor's Handbook: How to Profit from Early-Stage Investing by Gerald A. Benjamin, Joel Margulis. Publisher: Bloomberg Press (July 2001)

BARTERING RESOURCES

Online Resources

Barter.net at **www.barter.net**

Barter Consultants at **www.barterconsultants.com**

Barter It Online at **www.barteritonline.com**

Empowered Barter at **www.empoweredbarter.com/**

U-Exchange at **www.u-exchange.com**

IRS rules on bartering at **www.irs.gov/taxtopics/tc420.html**

BUSINESS PLAN RESOURCES

Online Resources

BPlans at **www.bplans.com**

Business Confidant at **www.businessconfidant.com**

Business-Plan at **www.business-plan.com**

Bulletproof Business Plans at
www.bulletproofbizplans.com

HJ Ventures at **http://hjventures.com/**

Business Plan at **www.business-plan.com** (offers Spanish
language books and software)

Megadox legal forms at **www.megadox.com/
documents.php/97**

Other Resources

*Anatomy of a Business Plan, 6th Ed.: A Step-by-Step Guide to
Building a Business and Securing Your Company's Future
(Anatomy of a Business Plan)* by Linda Pinson. Publisher:
Dearborn Trade, a Kaplan Professional Company;
6th Edition (November 1, 2004)

*Business Plans That Win $$$: Lessons from the MIT Enterprise
Forum* by Stanley R. Rich. Publisher: Perennial Currents;
Reprint Edition (February 18, 1987)

Bankable Business Plans by Edward Rogoff, Edward G.
Rogoff, Jeff Bezos. Publisher: Texere; 1st Edition
(September 2, 2003)

Plan for Profitability!: How to Write a Strategic Business Plan by Lee E. Hargrave, Jr. Publisher: Four Seasons Publishers (June 1, 1999)

The Complete Book of Business Plans: Simple Steps to Writing a Powerful Business Plan (Small Business Sourcebooks) by Joseph A. Covello, Brian J. Hazelgren. Publisher: Sourcebooks (April 1, 1994)

BUSINESS STRUCTURE

Incorporating Your Business for Dummies by The Company Corporation (For Dummies Publisher)

TurboTax article "Should I Incorporate" at **www.turbotax.com/articles/ShouldIIncorporate.html**.

All Business Practical Guide to Incorporation at **www.allbusiness.com/guides/Incorporation.asp**

Legal Spring consumer-oriented advice at **www.legalspring.com**

Business Filings Incorporated at **www.bizfilings.com**

My Corporation at **www.mycorporation.com**

Corporate Creations at **www.corpcreations.com**

CREDIT BUREAU ADDRESSES

Equifax, Inc.
P.O. Box 740241
Atlanta, GA 30374
1-800-685-1111
www.equifax.com

Experian
P.O. Box 2104
Allen, Texas 75013-2104
1-888-397-3742
www.experian.com

TransUnion Corporation
Consumer Disclosure Center
2 Baldwin Place
P.O. Box 1000
Chester, PA 19022
1-800-888-4213
www.transunion.com

CREDIT REPORTING/SCORES

Bank Rate at **www.bankrate.com/brm/
credit_scoring_home.asp**

How Stuff Works—how credit scores work at
http://money.howstuffworks.com/credit-score.htm

DEBT FINANCING RESOURCES

Online Resources

Business Owner's Toolkit at **www.toolkit.cch.com**

CommermcialCapital.Info at **www.commercialcapital.info/ debt-finance.asp**

Missouri MarketMaker at **www.marketmaker.org/Library/ Debt_financing/Debt_Financing.htm**

The University Financing Foundation at **www.tuff.org/ debtfin.html**

Other Resources

Collateralized Debt Obligations and Structured Finance: New Developments in Cash and Synthetic Securitization by Janet M. Tavakoli. Publisher: John Wiley & Sons (August 15, 2003)

Collateralized Debt Obligations: Structures and Analysis by Laurie S. Goodman, Frank J. Fabozzi. Publisher: Wiley; 1st Edition (September 13, 2002)

DPO RESOURCES

Online Resources

Virtual Capital Group at **www.virtualcapitalgroup.com/ dposervices.html**

Venture Associates at **www.venturea.com/dpo.htm**

Go Public Today at **www.gopublictoday.com/services/ services-dpo.php**

Other Resources

Direct Public Offerings: The New Method for Taking Your Company Public by Drew Field. Publisher: Sourcebooks (April 1, 1997)

Raising Capital for Your Business: Through the Use of Private Placement Offerings, Direct Public Offerings & Small Corporate Offerings by Michael N. Brette. Publisher: Griffin Publishing Group (November 1, 1998)

A Very Public Offering: A Rebel's Story of Business Excess, Success, and Reckoning by Stephan Paternot. Publisher: Wiley; New Edition (September 20, 2002)

Build It Big: 101 Insider Secrets from Top Direct Selling Experts by Direct Selling Women's Alliance (DSWA). Publisher: Dearborn Trade, a Kaplan Professional Company (January 15, 2005)

EQUITY FINANCING RESOURCES

Online Resources

Business Owner's Toolkit at **www.toolkit.cch.com/text/P10_ 2100.asp**

American Capital at **www.american-capital.com/resources/ types_of_financing/equity.cfm**

Small Business Administration at **www.sba.gov/financing/ basics/equity.html**

Century Small Biz at **www.centurysmallbiz.com/learning_centers/sbc/text/P10_2100.asp**

CommercialCapital.Info at **www.commercialcapital.info/equity-finance.asp**

Other Resources

Keys to Mortgage Financing and Refinancing (Barron's Business Keys) by Jack P. Friedman, Jack C. Harris. Publisher: Barron's Educational Series; 3rd Edition (January 1, 2001)

Angel Financing: How to Find and Invest in Private Equity by Gerald A. Benjamin, Joel B. Margulis. Publisher: Wiley; 2nd Edition (October 19, 1999)

Angel Capital: How to Raise Early-Stage Private Equity Financing (Wiley Finance) by Gerald A. Benjamin, Joel B. Margulis. Publisher: John Wiley & Sons (January 28, 2005)

FEASIBILITY STUDY RESOURCES

Should I Start a New Business? at **www.mapnp.org/library/strt_org/prep.htm**

FINANCIAL STATEMENTS RESOURCES

Online Resources

Small Business Administration at **www.sba.gov/managing/financing/statement.html**

Securities and Exchange Commission at **www.sec.gov/investor/pubs/begfinstmtguide.htm**

Business Owner's Toolkit at **www.toolkit.cch.com/text/ P06_1570.asp**

Corporate Credit at **http://corporatecredit.biz/ ?source=overture&keyword=financial%20statement**

Other Resources

Financial Statements: A Step-by-Step Guide to Understanding and Creating Financial Reports by Thomas R. Ittelson. Publisher: Career Press; 1st Edition (February 1, 1998)

How to Use Financial Statements: A Guide to Understanding the Numbers by James Bandler. Publisher: McGraw-Hill; 1st Edition (June 1, 1994)

The Guide to Understanding Financial Statements by S. B. Costales. Publisher: McGraw-Hill; 2nd Edition (October 1, 1993)

Business Analysis and Valuation: Using Financial Statements, Text and Cases by Krishna G. Palepu, Paul M. Healy, Victor L. Bernard. Publisher: South-Western College Pub; 3rd Edition (July 31, 2003)

GENERAL BUSINESS FINANCING INFORMATION

LiveCapital at **www.livecapital.com**

INDUSTRY DEMOGRAPHICS AND RESEARCH

Biz Miner at **www.bizminer.com**

Small Business Administration at **www.sba.gov/ starting_business/marketing/research.html**

IPO RESOURCES

Online Resources

IPO Home by Renaissance Capital at **www.ipohome.com**

Hoovers at **www.hoovers.com**

IPO Monitor at **www.ipomonitor.com**

Mr. Economist at **www.mreconomist.com**

Sharebuilder at **www.sharebuilder.com/sharebuilder/ ipocenter/Index.asp**

Other Resources

The Ernst & Young Guide to the IPO Value Journey by Stephen C. Blowers, Peter H. Griffith, and Thomas L. Milan. Publisher: Wiley; 1st Edition (October 8, 1999)

IPOs for Everyone: The 12 Secrets of Investing in IPOs by Linda R. Killian, Kathleen Shelton Smith, William K. Smith, Linda R. Killian, William K. Smith. Publisher: Wiley; 1st Edition (February 15, 2001)

LEVERAGE RESOURCES

Online Resources

Investopedia at **www.investopedia.com/terms/l/ leverage.asp**

Leverage Magazine at **www.leveragemag.com.au/**

Joint Venture for Profit at **http://jointventureforprofit.com/ leverage/**

Carole E. Scott, Professor of Economics at the State University of West Georgia at **www.westga. edu/~bquest/1998/leverage.html**

Business Owner's Toolkit at **www.toolkit.cch.com/ text/P06_7540.asp**

Other Resources

Optimize Now (or else!): How to Leverage Processes and Information to Achieve Enterprise Optimization (and Avoid Enterprise Extinction) by David M. Fisher. Publisher: iUniverse, Inc. (December 22, 2003)

Creating Strategic Leverage: Matching Company Strengths with Market Opportunities by Milind M. Lele. Publisher: Wiley; 1st Edition (December 11, 1991)

Leverage: A Key to Success and Wealth by Ron D. Pate. Publisher: VP Publishing, LLC (May 2004)

Loan Glossary

Find terms at **www.businesstown.com/finance/ money-glossary.asp**

LOAN PROPOSAL RESOURCES

Online Resources

Circle Lending at **www.circlelending.com/businessbuilder/ bb.loanCreatorInfo.asp**

DuPont Omni at **http://dupont.huggconsulting.com/ ibanking/preparing_loan_proposal.htm**

Lending America at **www.lendingamerica.com**

The Business Advisor Report at **www.mbwcpa.com/ BAR%20Preparing%20Loan%20Proposal.htm**

Other Resources

The Action Guide to Government Grants, Loans, and Giveaways by George Chelekis. Publisher: Perigee; Revised Edition (February 1, 1993)

2006 Guide to Federal Grants and Government Assistance to Small Business: Catalog of Federal Domestic Assistance, Loans, Grants, Surplus Equipment, SBA, GSA, SEC Information for Entrepreneurs, Startup Kit, Loan Programs, Financing, Law, Regulations, Reports, Workbooks – Applying for Federal Assistance (Two CD-ROM set) by U.S. Government. Publisher: Progressive Management; 1st Edition (September 3, 2005)

RESEARCH METHODS

Web Surveyor at **www.websurveyor.com**

SBA FINANCING RESOURCES

Online Resources

Small Business Administration at **www.sba.gov/financing**

Sharpe Finance at **www.sharpefinance.com/ sbafinancing.htm**

New Horizon Business Services at **www.newhorizon.org/NHBS/sba.htm**

Federal Funding Sources at **www.federalfundingsources.com/gt/info.htm**

Business Lenders at **www.businesslenders.com/?keyword=sba%20financing**

Small Biz Partners at **www.smallbizpartners.com**

Other Resources

21st Century Complete Guide to the Small Business Administration (SBA): Comprehensive Information for Entrepreneurs with the SBA Library of Documents, Forms, Startup Kit, Loan Programs and Financing, Laws and Regulations, and More by Small Business Administration. Publisher: Progressive Management (August 20, 2002)

2006 Guide to Federal Grants and Government Assistance to Small Business: Catalog of Federal Domestic Assistance, Loans, Grants, Surplus Equipment, SBA, GSA, SEC Information for Entrepreneurs, Startup Kit, Loan Programs, Financing, Law, Regulations, Reports, Workbooks – Applying for Federal Assistance (Two CD-ROM set) by U.S. Government. Publisher: Progressive Management; 1st Edition (September 3, 2005)

The SBA Loan Book by Charles H. Green. Publisher: Adams Media Corporation; 1st Edition (September 1, 1999)

STATE-BY-STATE
DIRECTORY OF SBA DISTRICT OFFICES

Alaska

U.S. Small Business Administration District Office
222 W. 8th Ave., Room #67
Anchorage, AK 99501
(907) 271-4022

Alabama

U.S. Small Business Administration District Office
2121 8th Ave. North, Suite #200
Birmingham, AL 35203-2398
(205) 731-1344

Arkansas

U.S. Small Business Administration District Office
320 W. Capital Ave., Room #601
Little Rock, AR 72201
(501) 378-5871

Arizona

U.S. Small Business Administration District Office
2005 N. Central Ave., 5th Floor
Phoenix, AZ 85004
(602) 379-3737

California

U.S. Small Business Administration District Office
2719 N. Air Fresno Dr.
Fresno, CA 93727-1547
(209) 487-5189

U.S. Small Business Administration District Office
330 N. Grand Blvd.
Glendale, CA 91203
(213) 894-2956

U.S. Small Business Administration District Office
901 W. Civic Center Dr., Room #160
Santa Ana, CA 92703
(714) 836-2494

U.S. Small Business Administration District Office
880 Front St., Suite #4-S-29
San Diego, CA 92188
(619) 557-5440

U.S. Small Business Administration District Office
211 Main St., 4th Floor
San Francisco, CA 94105-1988
(415) 974-0649

Colorado
U.S. Small Business Administration District Office
721 19th St., Room #407
Denver, CO 80202-2599
(303) 844-2607

Connecticut
U.S. Small Business Administration District Office
330 Main St., 2nd Floor
Hartford, CT 06106
(860) 240-4700

District of Columbia
U.S. Small Business Administration District Office
1111 18th St. NW, 6th Floor
Washington, DC 20036
(202) 634-1500

Florida
U.S. Small Business Administration District Office
1320 S. Dixie Highway, Suite #501
Coral Gables, FL 33146
(305) 536-5521

U.S. Small Business Administration District Office
7825 Baymeadows Way, Suite #100B
Jacksonville, FL 32256-7504
(904) 443-1950

Georgia
U.S. Small Business Administration District Office
1720 Peachtree Rd. NW, 6th Floor
Athens, GA 30309
(404) 347-4326

Hawaii
U.S. Small Business Administration District Office
300 Ala Moana Blvd., Room #2213
Honolulu, HI 96850
(808) 541-2990

Idaho
U.S. Small Business Administration District Office
1020 Main St., Suite #209
Boise, ID 83702
(208) 334-1696

Iowa

> U.S. Small Business Administration District Office
> 373 Collins Rd. NE, Room #100
> Cedar Rapids, IA 52402-3118
> (319) 399-2571

> U.S. Small Business Administration District Office
> 210 Walnut St., Room #749
> Des Moines, IA 50309
> (515) 284-4422

Illinois

> U.S. Small Business Administration District Office
> 219 S. Deerborn St., Room #437
> Chicago, IL 60604-1779
> (312) 353-4528

Indiana

> U.S. Small Business Administration District Office
> 575 N. Pennsylvania St., Room #578
> Indianapolis, IN 46204-1584
> (317) 226-7272

Kansas

> U.S. Small Business Administration District Office
> 110 E. Waterman St., 1st Floor
> Wichita, KS 67202
> (316) 269-6571

Kentucky

> U.S. Small Business Administration District Office
> 600 M.L. King, Jr. Pl., Room #188
> Louisville, KY 40202
> (502) 582-5976

Louisiana
> U.S. Small Business Administration District Office
> 1661 Canal St., Suite #2000
> New Orleans, LA 70112
> (504) 589-6685

Maine
> U.S. Small Business Administration District Office
> 40 Western Ave., Room #512
> Augusta, ME 04330
> (207) 622-8378

Maryland
> U.S. Small Business Administration District Office
> 10 N. Calvert St., 3rd Floor
> Baltimore, MD 21202
> (301) 962-4392

Massachusetts
> U.S. Small Business Administration District Office
> 10 Causeway St., Room #265
> Boston, MA 02222-1093
> (617) 565-5590

Michigan
> U.S. Small Business Administration District Office
> 477 Michigan Ave., Room #515
> Detroit, MI 48226
> (313) 226-6075

Minnesota
> U.S. Small Business Administration District Office
> 100 N. 6th St., Suite #610
> Minneapolis, MN 55403-1563
> (612) 370-2324

Mississippi

> U.S. Small Business Administration District Office
> 101 W. Capital St., Suite #322
> Jackson, MS 39269-0396

Missouri

> U.S. Small Business Administration District Office
> 1103 Grand Ave., 6th Floor
> Kansas City, MO 64106
> (816) 374-3419

> U.S. Small Business Administration District Office
> 815 Olive St., Room #242
> St. Louis, MO 63101
> (314) 539-6600

Montana

> U.S. Small Business Administration District Office
> 301 S. Park, Room #528
> Helena, MT 59626
> (406) 449-5381

Nebraska

> U.S. Small Business Administration District Office
> 11145 Mill Valley Rd.
> Omaha, NE 68154
> (402) 221-4691

Nevada

> U.S. Small Business Administration District Office
> 301 E. Stewart St., Room #301
> Las Vegas, NV 89125
> (702) 388-6611

New Jersey
    U.S. Small Business Administration District Office
    60 Park Pl., 4th Floor
    Newark, NJ 07102
    (201) 645-2434

New Mexico
    U.S. Small Business Administration District Office
    5000 Marble Ave. NE, Room #320
    Albuquerque, NM 87100
    (505) 262-6171

New York
    U.S. Small Business Administration District Office
    26 Federal Plaza, Room #3100
    New York, NY 10278
    (212) 264-4355

    U.S. Small Business Administration District Office
    100 S. Clinton St., Room #1071
    Syracuse, NY 13260
    (315) 423-5383

North Carolina
    U.S. Small Business Administration District Office
    222 S. Church St., Room #300
    Charlotte, NC 28202
    (704) 371-6563

North Dakota
    U.S. Small Business Administration District Office
    657 2nd Ave. N, Room #218
    Fargo, ND 58108-3086
    (701) 239-5131

Ohio

U.S. Small Business Administration District Office
1240 E. 9th St., Room #317
Cleveland, OH 44199
(216) 522-4180

U.S. Small Business Administration District Office
85 Marconi Blvd., Room #512
Columbus, OH 43215
(614) 469-6860

Oklahoma

U.S. Small Business Administration District Office
200 NW 5th St., Suite #670
Oklahoma City, OK 73102
(405) 231-4301

Oregon

U.S. Small Business Administration District Office
222 SW Columbia, Suite #500
Portland, OR 97201-6605
(503) 326-2682

Pennsylvania

U.S. Small Business Administration District Office
475 Allendale Rd., Suite #210
King of Prussia, PA 19406
(215) 962-3846

U.S. Small Business Administration District Office
960 Penn Ave., 5th Floor
Pittsburgh, PA 15222
(412) 644-2780

Rhode Island

U.S. Small Business Administration District Office
380 Westminster Mall, 5th Floor
Providence, RI 02903
(401) 528-4561

South Carolina

U.S. Small Business Administration District Office
1835 Assembly St., Room #358
Columbia, SC 29202
(803) 765-5376

South Dakota

U.S. Small Business Administration District Office
101 S. Main Ave., Suite #101
Sioux Falls, SD 57102
(605) 336-4231

Tennessee

U.S. Small Business Administration District Office
50 Vantage Way, 2nd Floor
Nashville, TN 37228-1500
(615) 736-5850

Texas

U.S. Small Business Administration District Office
1100 Commerce St., Room #3C-36
Dallas, TX 75242
(214) 767-0605

U.S. Small Business Administration District Office
10737 Gateway W, Suite #320
El Paso, TX 79902
(915) 541-7586

U.S. Small Business Administration District Office
2525 Murworth St., Suite #112
Houston, TX 77054
(713) 660-4401

U.S. Small Business Administration District Office
7400 Bianco Rd., Suite #200
San Antonio, TX 78216
(512) 229-4535

Utah

U.S. Small Business Administration District Office
125 S. State St., Room #2237
Salt Lake City, UT 84138
(801) 524-5800

Vermont

U.S. Small Business Administration District Office
87 State St., Room #205
Montpelier, VT 05602
(802) 828-4474

Virginia

U.S. Small Business Administration District Office
400 N. 8th St., Room #2237
Richmond, VA 23240
(804) 771-2617

Washington

U.S. Small Business Administration District Office
915 Second Ave., Room #1792
Seattle, WA 98174-1088
(206) 442-5534

U.S. Small Business Administration District Office
W. 601 First Ave., 10th Floor
Spokane, WA 99204
(509) 353-2807

West Virginia
U.S. Small Business Administration District Office
168 W. Main St., 5th Floor
Clarksburg, WV 26301
(304) 623-5631

Wisconsin
U.S. Small Business Administration District Office
212 E. Washington Ave., Room #213
Madison, WI 53703
(608) 264-5261

Wyoming
U.S. Small Business Administration District Office
100 East B. St., Room #4001
Casper, WY 82602
(307) 261-5761

Puerto Rico
U.S. Small Business Administration District Office
Carlos Chardon Ave., Room #691
Hato Rey, PR 00918
(809) 753-4002

SMALL BUSINESS DEVELOPMENT & SUPPORT

SCORE at **www.score.org**

Association for Enterprise Opportunity at **www.microenterpriseworks.org**—support for small (five employees or fewer) businesses with startup costs of $35,000 or less

Entrepreneur at **www.entrepreneur.com**—offers general business and restaurant-specific guidance

Bibliomaven at **www.bibliomaven.com/businessjournals**—locate state and local business journals

TRAINING CLASSES, SEMINARS, WORKSHOPS, AND WEB-BASED EDUCATION

NxLevel at **www.nxlevel.org**—free or low-cost business plan writing and entrepreneurial support training

FastTrack at **www.fasttrac.org**—Spanish and English programs and information

VALUATION RESOURCES

Online Resources

Valuation Resources at **www.valuationresources.com**

Excel Business Tools valuation analysis at **www. excelbusinesstools.com/investval.htm**

Business Valuation Resources at **www.bvresources.com**

Business Valuation Services at **www.bus-valu.com**

Other Resources

The Small Business Valuation Book (Adams Expert Advice for Small Business) by Lawrence W. Tuller. Publisher: Adams Media Corporation; 1st Edition (March 1998)

The Business Valuation Book (with CD-ROM) by Scott Gabehart, Richard Brinkley. Publisher: American Management Association; CD-ROM Edition (June 15, 2002)

Valuing Small Businesses and Professional Practices (Art of M & A) by Shannon P. Pratt, Robert F. Reilly, Robert P. Schweihs. Publisher: McGraw-Hill; 3rd Edition (March 1, 1998)

Business Analysis and Valuation: Using Financial Statements, Text and Cases by Krishna G. Palepu, Paul M. Healy, Victor L. Bernard. Publisher: South-Western College Pub; 3rd Edition (July 31, 2003)

Valuation: Measuring and Managing the Value of Companies, 3rd Edition by McKinsey & Company Inc., Tom Copeland, Tim Koller, Jack Murrin. Publisher: Wiley; 3rd Edition (July 28, 2000)

Ballpark Business Valuation Software available at **www.bulletproofbizplans.com/BallPark**

VENTURE CAPITAL RESOURCES

Online Resources

National Venture Capital Association at **www.nvca.org**

Global Venture Site at **www.globalventuresite.com**

Funding Post at **www.fundingpost.com/entre/ entsignupA1.asp?refer=V-VenCap**

VCA Online at **www.vcaonline.com**

V-Finance at **www.vfinance.com**

Other Resources

Deal Terms—The Finer Points of Venture Capital Deal Structures, Valuations, Term Sheets, Stock Options and Getting Deals Done by Alex Wilmerding, Aspatore Books Staff, Aspatore.com. Publisher: Aspatore Books (January 1, 2003)

Structuring Venture Capital, Private Equity, and Entrepreneurial Transactions, 2004 Edition by Jack S. Levin, Martin D. Ginsburg (Editor), Donald E. Rocap (Editor). Publisher: Aspen Publishers (April 2004)

Venture Capital Due Diligence: A Guide to Making Smart Investment Choices and Increasing Your Portfolio Returns by Justin J. Camp. Publisher: Wiley; 1st Edition (January 18, 2002)

STATE-BY-STATE DIRECTORY
OF VENTURE CAPITAL CLUBS AND NETWORKS

Alabama

Birmingham Venture Club
Birmingham Chamber of Commerce
P.O. Box 10127
Birmingham, AL 35202
(202) 323-5461

Arizona

Arizona Venture Capital Conference
Phoenix Chamber of Commerce
201 N. Central Ave., Suite #2700
Phoenix, AZ 85073
(602) 495-6488

Arkansas

Venture Capital Investors, Inc.
400 W. Capital Ave.
Little Rock, AR 72201-3441
(501) 372-5900

California

CalTech/MIT Enterprise Forum
Industrial Relations Center 1-90
Pasadena, CA 91125
(626) 395-4041

Central Coast MIT Enterprise Forum, Inc.
Interlink Electronics
546 Flynn Rd.
Camarillo, CA 93012
(805) 484-8855

Community Entrepreneurs Association
P.O. Box 9838
San Rafael, CA 94912
(415) 435-4461

Los Angeles Venture Association
626 Santa Monica Blvd. Suite #129
Santa Monica, CA 90401-1066
(310) 450-9544

MIT Enterprise Forum of the Bay Area, Inc.
(408) 323-2255
www.vlab.org

MIT Enterprise Forum of San Diego
Executive Outsourcing International
16528 Calle Pulido, Suite #101
San Diego, CA 92128
(619) 236-8940

Northern California Venture Forum
International Capital Resources
388 Market St., Suite #500
San Francisco, CA 94111
(415) 296-2519
www.icrnet.com

Orange Coast Venture Group
23011 Moulton Parkway, Suite #F-2
Laguna Hills, CA 92653
(714) 859-3646

San Diego Venture Group
750 B St., Suite #2400
San Diego, CA 92101
(619) 231-8055
www.sdvgroup.org

The Springboard Program
CONNECT-UCSD, MS-0176F
La Jolla, CA 92093-0649
(619) 534-6114
www.connect.org/connect

Colorado

Rockies Venture Club
190 E 9th Ave., Suite #320
Denver, CO 80203
(303) 831-4174
www.metzger.com/rvc

Venture Capital in the Rockies
KPMG Peat Marwick
707 17th St., Suite #2300
Denver, CO 80202
(303) 296-2323

Connecticut

Connecticut Venture Group
425 Katona Dr.
Fairfield, CT 06430
(203) 333-3284

MIT Enterprise Forum of Connecticut
1 American Row
Hartford, CT 06103
(860) 251-5000

Delaware

Delaware Entrepreneurs' Forum
P.O. Box 278
Yorklyn, DE 19736
(302) 652-4241

Florida

Central Florida Innovation Corporation
12424 Research Parkway, Suite #350
Orlando, FL 32826
(407) 277-5411

North Florida Venture Capital Network
7400 Bay Meadows Way, Suite #201
Jacksonville, FL 32256
(904) 730-4726

Florida Venture Forum
Florida International University
2600 Douglas Rd., Suite #311
Coral Gables, FL 33134
(305) 446-5060
www.fiu.edu/~fvf

The Founders Forum
Downtown Office Center
1900 South Harbor City Blvd.
Melbourne, FL 32901
(407) 984-1900

Gainesville Area Innovation Network
Southern Technology Applications Center
P.O. Box 13442
Gainesville, FL 32604
(352) 466-4387

Gold Coast Venture Capital Club
11401-A W. Palmetto Park Rd., Suite #202
Boca Raton, FL 33428
(561) 488-4505

Georgia

Network for Business Acquisitions and Investments
3873 Roswell Rd., Suite #4
Atlanta, GA 30342
(404) 261-2434

Hawaii

Hawaii Venture Capital Association
805 Kainui Dr.
Kailua, HI 96734-2025
(808) 262-7329

Idaho

Rocky Mountain Venture Group
Department of Energy
2300 North Yellowstone
Idaho Falls, ID 83401
(208) 526-1181

Illinois

MIT Venture Capital Forum of Chicago
8 S. Michigan Ave., Suite #1000
Chicago, IL 60603
(312) 782-4951

Indiana

Entrepreneurs' Alliance of Indiana
P.O. Box 90096
Indianapolis, IN 46240-1211
(317) 216-8290

Indiana Private Investor's Network
216 W. Allen St.
Bloomington, IN 47403
(812) 339-8937

Michiana Investment Network
Small Business Development Center
300 N. Michigan St.
South Bend, IN 46601
(219) 282-4350

Venture Club of Indiana
P.O. Box 40872
Indianapolis, IN 46240-0872
(317) 253-1244

Iowa

Venture Network of Iowa
Iowa Department of Economic Development
200 E. Grand St.
Des Moines, IA 50309
(515) 242-4776

Kansas

Kansas Technology Enterprise Corporation
214 SW 6th Ave., 1st Floor
Topeka, KS 66603-3719
(785) 296-5272

Kentucky

Venture Club of Louisville
304 W. Liberty, Suite #301
Louisville, KY 40202
(502) 589-6868

Louisiana

The Venture Network
601 Poydras St., Suite #1700
New Orleans, LA 70130
(504) 527-6936

Maine

Maine Investment Exchange
Maine and Company
120 Exchange St.
Portland, ME 04101
(207) 871-0234

Maryland

Baltimore-Washington Investment Group
Dingman Center for Entrepreneurship
The Robert H. Smith School of Business
4361 Van Munching Hall
The University of Maryland
College Park, MD 20742-1815
(301) 405-2144

Massachusetts

MIT Enterprise Forum, Inc.
28 Carleton St.
Building E32-330
Cambridge, MA 02139
(617) 253-0015
www.mitforum-canbridge.org

128 Venture Capital Group
Bedford Rd.
Lincoln, MA 01773
(781) 259-8776

Technology Capital Network at MIT
P.O. Box 425936
Cambridge, MA 02142
(617) 253-7163

Venture-Preneurs Network
85 East India Row, Suite 23B
Boston, MA 02110
(617) 720-1525
www.venturepreneurs.com

Michigan

Southeastern Michigan Venture group
20630 Harper Ave., Suite #103
Harper Woods, MI 48225
(313) 886-2331

Traverse Bay Enterprise Forum
P.O. Box 506
Traverse City, MI 49685-0506
(616) 929-5017

Venture Center, Inc.
P.O. Box 27186
Lansing, MI 48909-7186
(517) 337-2672
www.bus.msu.edu/venture/

Minnesota

The Collaborative
10 S. Fifth St., Suite #415
Minneapolis, MN 55402-1004
(612) 338-3828

Missouri

Missouri Venture Forum
917 Locust St., 5th Floor
St. Louis, MO 63101
(314) 621-2683

Nebraska

Nebraska Center for Entrepreneurship
CBA 209
University of Nebraska
Lincoln, NE 68558-0487
(402) 472-3353

Nevada

Venture Capital in the Rockies
KPMG Peat Marwick
707 17th St., Suite #2300
Denver, CO 80202
(303) 296-2323

New Hampshire

Nashua Breakfast Club
R. Morley, Inc.
586 Nashua St., Suite #56
Milford, NH 03055
(603) 878-4365

New Jersey

Venture Association of New Jersey
P.O. Box 1982
Morristown, NJ 07962-1982
(973) 267-4200
www.vanj.com

New Mexico
Venture Capital in the Rockies
KPMG Peat Marwick
707 17th St., Suite #2300
Denver, CO 80202
(303) 296-2323

New York
Western New York Venture Association
Baird Research Park
1576 Sweet Home Rd.
Amherst, NY 14228
(716) 636-3626

Long Island Venture Group
Business Development Center, Room #217
145 Hofstra University
Hempstead, NY 11549-1450
(516) 463-6326

MIT Enterprise Forum of New York City, Inc.
420 Lexington Ave., Room #2400
New York, NY 10170
(212) 681-1112

North Carolina
Council for Entrepreneurial Development
104 Alexander Dr.
P.O. Box 13353
Research Triangle Park, NC 27709-3353
(919) 549-7500

North Dakota

North Dakota Development Fund
1833 E. Bismarck Expressway
Bismarck, ND 58504-6708
(701) 328-5310

Ohio

Greater Cincinnati Venture Association
Greater Cincinnati Chamber of Commerce
441 Vine St.
300 Carew Tower
Cincinnati, OH 45202-2812

Ohio Venture Association
1127 Euclid Ave., Suite #343
Cleveland, OH 44115
(216) 566-8884

Oklahoma

Entrepreneurs of Tulsa
401 S. Boston
Mid-Continent Tower, 18th Floor, Suite #1810
Tulsa, OK 74103-4018
(918) 582-6131

Oregon

Oregon Enterprise Forum
2611 SW Third Ave., Suite #200
Portland, OR 97201
(503) 222-2270

Pennsylvania

Greater Philadelphia Venture Group
200 South Broad St., Suite #700
Philadelphia, PA 19102-3896
(215) 790-3601
www.gpcc.com

Loosely Organized Retired Executives
Versus Corporation
5 Radnor Corporate Center
100 Matsonford Rd., Suite #520
Radnor, PA 19087
(610) 964-8452

MIT Enterprise Forum of Pittsburgh, Inc.
Berthold Systems, Inc.
101 Corporation Dr.
Aliquippa, PA 15001-4863
(724) 378-1926

Pennsylvania Private Investors Group
3625 Market St., Suite #200
Philadelphia, PA 19104
(800) 288-3302

Rhode Island

Brown University Venture Forum
P.O. Box 1949
Providence, RI 02912
(401) 863-3528

Hope Investors
2 Charles St.
Providence, RI 02904
(401) 861-0320

South Carolina

Dare to Deal-Southeast Capital Connection
Center for Entrepreneurship, College of Charleston
66 George St.
Charleston, SC 29424-0001

South Dakota

Dakota Ventures
P.O. Box 8194
Rapid City, SD 57709
(605) 348-8441

Texas

MIT Enterprise Forum of Dallas-Forth Worth, Inc.
Interactive Creations
1701 West Northwest Highway, Suite #220
Grapevine, TX 76051
(817) 424-5638

MIT Enterprise Forum of Texas, Inc.
711 Louisiana St., Suite #2900
Houston, TX 77002-2781
(713) 221-1303

Utah

Utah Venture Capital Conference
Wayne Brown Institute
P.O. Box 2135
Salt Lake City, UT 84110-2135
(801) 595-1181

Vermont

Vermont Investor's Forum
Green Mountain Capital
RD 1, Box 1503
Waterbury, VT 05676
(802) 244-8981

Virginia

Hampton Roads Private Investor Network
Small Business Development Center of
   Hampton Roads, Inc.
400 Bank St.
Norfolk, VA 23501
(757) 825-2957

MIT Enterprise Forum of Washington-Baltimore, Inc.
P.O. Box 26203
Arlington, VA 22215
(703) 365-9023

Private Investors' Network
402 Maple Ave. W
Vienna, VA 22180
(703) 255-4930

Richmond Venture Capital Club
1407 Huguenot Rd.
Midlothian, VA 23113
(804) 794-1117

Washington

Northwest Venture Group
P.O. Box 21693
Seattle, WA 98111-3693
(425) 746-1973

MIT Enterprise Forum of the Northwest, Inc.
1319 Decker Ave. N., #370
Seattle, WA 98109
(206) 283-9595
www.mitwa.org

Wisconsin

Wisconsin Venture Network
P.O. Box 92093
Milwaukee, WI 53202
(414) 224-5988

Wisconsin Innovation Network Foundation
P.O. Box 71
Madison, WI 53701-0071
(608) 256-8348

Wyoming

Venture Capital in the Rockies
KPMG Peat Marwick
707 17th St., Suite #2300
Denver, CO 80202
(303) 296-2323

INDEX

DID YOU BORROW THIS COPY?

More Great Titles for **SMALL BUSINESS**

HOW TO WRITE A GREAT BUSINESS PLAN FOR YOUR SMALL BUSINESS IN 60 MINUTES OR LESS: WITH COMPANION CD-ROM

The importance of a comprehensive, thoughtful business plan cannot be overemphasized. Much hinges on it: outside funding; credit from suppliers; management of your operation and finances; promotion and marketing of your business; achievement of your goals and objectives, yet many small businesses never take the time to prepare one. Now it's easy—and you can do it in less than an hour. This new book and companion CD-ROM will demonstrate how to construct a current and pro-forma balance sheet, an income statement, and a cash flow analysis. You will learn to allocate resources properly, handle unforeseen complications, and make good business decisions. The CD-ROM file (written in Microsoft Word) allows you to simply plug in your own information while providing specific and organized information about your company and how you will repay borrowed money; additionally, it informs sales personnel, suppliers, and others about your operations and goals. 288 pages.   **Item # GBP-01 $39.95**

2,001 INNOVATIVE WAYS TO SAVE YOUR COMPANY THOUSANDS BY REDUCING COSTS: A COMPLETE GUIDE TO CREATIVE COST CUTTING AND BOOSTING PROFIT

This new book is full of practical advice on thousands of innovative ways to cut costs in every area of your business. Not only is the idea presented, but the pertinent information is provided for action, such as contact information and Web sites for companies, products, or services recommended. We spent thousands of hours interviewing, e-mailing, and communicating with hundreds of today's most successful small business managers and owners. This book is a compilation of their secrets and proven successful ideas. 288 pages.   **Item # IWS-02 $21.95**

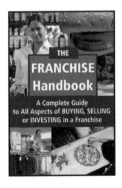

THE FRANCHISE HANDBOOK: A COMPLETE GUIDE TO ALL ASPECTS OF BUYING, SELLING OR INVESTING IN A FRANCHISE

According to the U.S. Department of Commerce, buying a franchise is the average person's most viable avenue to owning a business. As a successful small business owner, franchising your existing business plan to others is perhaps your fastest way to growth and enormous profits. This book will be a great resource for both prospective franchisees and franchisors as it explains in detail what the franchise system entails and the precise benefits it offers to both parties.

You will learn franchising advantages and disadvantages, how to develop or purchase a winning concept, how to choose a business franchise that fits your personal style and financial goals, how to develop forecasts and budgets, and how to estimate startup costs. The book also covers managing daily operations, attracting and keeping customers, hiring employees and training staff, securing financing, legal agreements, offerings, markets, real estate, cost control, marketing, international franchising, as well as federal and state franchise regulations. Ensure friendly franchisor/franchisee relationships and build a fortune franchising your own business concept. 288 pages.   **Item # TFH-01 $39.95**

To order call toll-free **800-814-1132**
or visit **www.atlantic-pub.com**

Get the most from your EMPLOYEES

DESIGN YOUR OWN EFFECTIVE EMPLOYEE HANDBOOK: HOW TO MAKE THE MOST OF YOUR STAFF: WITH COMPANION CD-ROM

Our Employee Handbook Template is the ideal solution to produce your own handbook in less than an hour. The companion CD-ROM in MS Word contains the template that you can easily edit for our own purposes; essentially fill in the blank. The book discusses various options you may have in developing the policies. Our employee handbook has been edited and approved by lawyers specializing in employment law. Developing your own handbook now couldn't be easier or less expensive! 288 pages.
Item # GEH-02 $39.95

365 ANSWERS ABOUT HUMAN RESOURCES FOR THE SMALL BUSINESS OWNER: WHAT EVERY MANAGER NEEDS TO KNOW ABOUT WORKPLACE LAW

Finally there is a complete and up-to-date resource for the small business owner. Tired of high legal and consulting fees? This new book is your answer. Detailed are over 300 common questions employers have about employees and the law; it's like having an employment attorney on your staff. Topics include: equal employment opportunity, age discrimination, Americans with Disabilities Act (ADA), unacceptable job performance, termination, substance abuse, drug and alcohol testing, safety, harassment, compensation policies, job classifications, recordkeeping, overtime, employee performance evaluations, wage and salary reviews, payroll, and much more. 288 pages.
Item # HRM-02 $21.95

HOW TO HIRE, TRAIN & KEEP THE BEST EMPLOYEES FOR YOUR SMALL BUSINESS: WITH COMPANION CD-ROM

You will learn the fundamentals of sound hiring, how to identify high-performance candidates, and how to spot evasions. Innovative step-by-step descriptions of how to recruit, interview, hire, train, and KEEP the best people for every position in your organization. The book is filled to the brim with innovative and fun training ideas (that cost little or nothing) and ideas for increasing employee involvement and enthusiasm. When you get your employees involved and enthused, you will keep them interested and working with you, not against you. With the help of this book, get started today on building your workplace into one that inspires employees to do excellent work because they really want to! 288 pages.
Item # HTK-02 $29.95

501+ GREAT INTERVIEW QUESTIONS FOR EMPLOYERS AND THE BEST ANSWERS FOR PROSPECTIVE EMPLOYEES

For anyone who hires employees, this is a must-have book. It is also essential for anyone searching for a new job or going on a job interview. Hiring new employees to fill a job vacancy is one of any manager's most important responsibilities. This book contains a wide variety of carefully worded questions that will help make the employee search easier. It will help you determine a candidate's personality type, the type of work he or she is best suited for, and if the person will mesh with your existing employees and workplace. Once you learn the right questions to ask, you'll get the best employees. For the prospective employee, learn how to sell yourself and get the job you want! From this new book you will learn how to answer the toughest interview questions by being fully prepared and understanding what employers are looking for. 288 pages.
Item # 501-02 $24.95

To order call toll-free **800-814-1132** or visit **www.atlantic-pub.com**

Learn to take advantage of the **INTERNET**

ONLINE MARKETING SUCCESS STORIES: INSIDER SECRETS FROM THE EXPERTS WHO ARE MAKING MILLIONS ON THE INTERNET TODAY

Standing out in the turmoil of today's Internet marketplace is a major challenge. There are many books and courses on Internet marketing, but this is the only book that will provide you with insider secrets because we asked the marketing experts who make their living on the Internet every day—and they talked. *Online Marketing Success Stories* will give you real-life examples of how successful businesses market their products online. The information is so useful that you can read a page and put the idea into action—today! Learn the most efficient ways to bring consumers to your site, get visitors to purchase, how to up-sell, oversights to avoid, and how to steer clear of years of disappointment. 288 pages. **Item # OMS-02 $21.95**

EBAY INCOME: HOW ANYONE OF ANY AGE, LOCATION AND/OR BACKGROUND CAN BUILD A HIGHLY PROFITABLE ONLINE BUSINESS WITH EBAY

Start making money on eBay today. The book starts with a complete overview of how eBay works. Then the book will guide you through the whole process of creating the auction and auction strategies, photography, writing copy, text and formatting, managing auctions, shipping, collecting payments, registering, About Me page, sources for merchandise, multiple sales, programming tricks, PayPal, accounting, creating marketing, merchandising, managing e-mail lists, advertising plans, taxes and sales tax, best time to list items and for how long, sniping programs, international customers, opening a storefront, electronic commerce, buy-it now pricing, keywords, Google marketing, and eBay secrets; everything you will ever need to get started making money on eBay. 288 pages. **Item # EBY-01 $24.95**

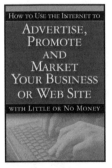

HOW TO USE THE INTERNET TO ADVERTISE, PROMOTE AND MARKET YOUR BUSINESS OR WEB SITE WITH LITTLE OR NO MONEY

Interested in promoting your business and/or Web site, but don't have the big budget for traditional advertising? This new book will show you how to build, promote, and make money off of your Web site or brick and mortar store using the Internet, with minimal costs. Let us arm you with the knowledge you need to make your business a success! Learn how to generate more traffic for your site or store with hundreds of Internet marketing methods, including many free and low-cost promotions. This new book presents a comprehensive, hands-on, step-by-step guide for increasing Web site traffic and traditional store traffic by using hundreds of proven tips, tools, and techniques. 288 pages. **Item # HIA-01 $24.95**

THE EBAY SUCCESS CHRONICLES: SECRETS AND TECHNIQUES EBAY POWERSELLERS USE EVERY DAY TO MAKE MILLIONS

There are many books on eBay, but this is the only one that will provide you with insider secrets because we asked the PowerSeller experts who make their living on eBay every day—and they talked. We spent thousands of hours interviewing and e-mailing eBay PowerSellers. This book is a compilation of their secrets and proven successful ideas. If you are interested in learning hundreds of hints, tricks, and secrets on how to make money (or more money) on eBay, then this book is for you. Currently with over 430,000 sellers make a living off eBay, there is no reason you shouldn't become financially successful. This book will arm you with the knowledge to become an eBay PowerSeller. 288 pages. **Item # ESC-02 $21.95**

To order call toll-free **800-814-1132** or visit **www.atlantic-pub.com**

Optimize Your REAL ESTATE & INVESTING

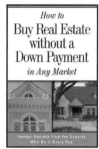